ALL THE WAY
TO
HEAVEN

ALL THE WAY TO HEAVEN

A SURPRISING FAITH JOURNEY

ELIZABETH SHERRILL

eagle

Bath, England

Copyright © 2002 by Elizabeth Sherrill

Published by Eagle Publishing Ltd, 6 Kestrel House, Mill Street, Trowbridge, Wilts BA14 8BE

Originally published by Fleming H. Revell
A division of Baker Book House Company
P.O. Box 6287, Grand Rapids, MI 49516-6287

British Library Cataloguing in Publication Data. A catalogue record for this book is available from the British Library.

Typeset by Eagle Publishing Ltd
Printed by Bookmarqe Ltd
ISBN 0 86347 574 4

Contents

The Secret   7

Heaven behind Me   17

Heaven around Me   77

Heaven before Me   135

All the way to heaven
is heaven,
for he said,
'I am the Way.'

Catherine of Siena

This book is about discovery – the discovery of a secret. It's the story of how heaven, which I used to think of as an imaginary realm-in-the-sky, has become more real to me than the ground beneath my feet. Real in the past, real for the future, and best of all, real right now. And the book is also an invitation. An invitation to us all to look back, to look ahead, and to look around, and keep discovering the secret for ourselves.

Saint Catherine's Secret

In the Italian city of Siena, I have a favourite place to stay. It's a small hostel just below the church of San Domenico. The no-frills rooms are small, and you have to go elsewhere even for a cup of coffee. What it offers is the best view in town. From the balcony I look across a ravine at the crenellated walls and towers of the medieval city.

Just below the balcony, however, is the site that means most to me. It's the birthplace of Catherine of Siena. *It's strange,* I think, gazing down at the narrow street where her father had his dye shop, *that this Roman Catholic saint should have so much to say to me* – not only a non-Catholic, but someone to whom the very concept of 'saints' was once an instant turnoff.

I get no help from the birthplace itself; the dye shop with the family home above it was redesigned as a shrine five hundred years ago. Some things, though, remain as Catherine knew them. San Domenico's is the parish church where she had her visions of heaven. I can still descend the steep-pitched street to the well at the foot of the hill where she went each day for water after her parents turned her into the family drudge for refusing an advantageous marriage. I follow her footsteps as she struggles up the slope with the heavy buckets.

It was only the first of the toils and conflicts that made up her life. As the Black Plague raged unchecked, most were afraid even to come near the victims. Catherine nursed them, consoled them, buried the dead with her own hands.

This was the fourteenth century, when Italian city-states waged bloody war on one another, and timorous popes abandoned Italy for seventy years. As Catherine's reputation spread, she was drawn into the tumultuous politics of her time, even travelling to the papal court in France to persuade the pope to return to Rome – only to see him followed by a pontiff so avaricious that cardinals held a second election, splitting Europe for decades between rival popes. Grief-stricken over the failures of the church, Catherine fell ill with what may have been infantile paralysis, and after weeks of agony, she died at the age of thirty-three.

A tragic life? On the contrary, said Catherine, her life was heaven on earth. '*All* the way to heaven is heaven,' she declared, 'for he said, "I am the Way."'

It wasn't some carefree soul basking in good fortune who reached this happy conclusion. It was a traveller on a hard and uphill road, who found that the journey with Jesus was heaven, whatever the outward circumstances.

Catherine's secret was to see her life as a love story. To receive each hour of each day, no matter how thankless and hard, as the perfect gift of the perfect Lover.

What if I could learn to do that! I think as I follow her steps through Siena's winding alleys. For since I encountered St Catherine, I've met others, people living in today's world, who have. Who've learned to see in the particulars of their lives, even in pain and loss, God's very personal wooing.

For fifty years, through books and through articles for *Guideposts* magazine, I've enjoyed seeking out and relating these true romances. Anyone's but my own. I've shied away from telling my own love story, excusing myself because I'm a 'private person'. What's to tell, anyway? Once when my husband, John, and I were living in England, a local paper ran a series on 'A Day in the Life'. *A day in the life* of a Queen's Guardsman. *A day in the life* of a Schoolteacher. A reporter interviewed me for *A day in the life* of a Writer – surely of all daily routines the dullest:

  8:10 sit at desk
  9:15 put on another pot of coffee
10:12 resharpen pencils
11:26 cross out everything written since 8:10

My work, it's true, has allowed me to meet people – some famous, some little known – with gripping stories to tell. Some of these are in this book.

But suppose God wants us to tell the everyday stories too!

Nothing is more important, writes Frederick Buechner in *Telling Secrets,* 'than that we keep track, you and I, of who we are and where we have come from and the people we have met along the way because it is precisely through these stories in all their particularity that God makes himself known most powerfully and personally'.

God making himself known . . . Perhaps this is the purpose of our separate stories in their endless variety. Perhaps heaven is where we will recount, each to the other, millions and billions of us, the story of our individual journey to that kingdom and what we learned of the King along the way.

The story of my particular journey began, as I suspect most do, long before I knew I was on a journey at all. Least of all did I know its destination. It's only looking back that I can make out the way I've come and see that all along, the way was Jesus.

The Homecoming

Thou has made us for thyself, O Lord, and our heart is restless until it rests in thee.

Augustine of Hippo

I stood at the railing of the boat deck, staring through the drizzle as the coast of England drew near. It was 1947. I was nineteen, a college junior headed for the University of Geneva in Switzerland, recently reopened to foreign students after the war. The *Queen Elizabeth* would dock at Southampton before crossing to France.

All along the railing homecoming passengers were pointing out landmarks through the mist. I took off my glasses and rubbed them again with a rain-soaked handkerchief. Land was on both sides of us now as we glided up the Narrows, the *Elizabeth*'s deep-throated horn blasting a continual warning to other ships. From fishing boats and cargo ships came answering toots and whistles as the world's largest ship steamed into home port. The man next to me at the railing, a morose-looking Englishman with the limp right sleeve of his raincoat tucked into his pocket, broke out with the first words he'd uttered: 'Couldn't raise this hullabaloo during the war. She had to creep in after dark. No lights. No horn.'

At Southampton the dock swarmed with stevedores and black-helmeted bobbies. As tugs eased the great ship into her berth, I gazed past the waterfront at the clustered rooftops of the town, war damage still evident in rubble-strewn lots.

And suddenly, unaccountably, I burst into tears.

The one-armed war veteran, as I took him to be, turned a startled face to me. 'It's all right, Miss. Civilians were moved inland.'

And then, as I continued to sob: 'Why, this is nothing, Miss! Wait till you see some of the spots Jerry really got to. Wait till you see London.'

But it wasn't the bombed-out blocks. For years I'd seen newsreels of devastation far worse than this. I stabbed at my eyes with the useless handkerchief, trying to explain . . . what? A reaction so strange, so totally illogical, that I didn't understand it myself.

In a well-meant effort to reassure me, my companion launched into an upbeat description of England's postwar recovery. Below us gangplanks were hoisted into place. Satisfied that he'd stopped the flow of tears, the man left to join the other disembarking passengers.

His kindness, however, was misplaced. The tears were not for sorrow but for joy. I was crying because I was home at last.

The sense of coming home to a place I'd never been . . .

Where could such a bizarre reaction have come from? It was my first trip anywhere overseas. What I could see of the town was foreign-looking – small houses, big gardens, cars of unfamiliar make travelling on the wrong side of narrow streets. Yet I recognised the place as though I'd been looking for it all my life.

Or – as though it had been looking for me. In some unfathomable way I had been found. And till that moment I had not known that I was lost . . .

Since then, I've returned to England many times, and always with that inexplicable sense of homecoming. Is it the books I grew up with, I've wondered – *Winnie the Pooh* and *Mary Poppins*, the Brontës, Shakespeare? Or could it be some kind of ancestral memory – those many-times-great-grandparents who came from England?

How to explain it, even arriving by plane, herded with hundreds of other half-asleep passengers through the anonymous corridors of Heathrow Airport: that swelling of joy, that welling of tears. *I belong! I belong!* The apologetic demur to sympathetic strangers: 'No, I'm all right. Really.'

Really all right, in a way I cannot explain, but which I've come to feel has a parallel in the life of the spirit. It was so similar, that spiritual homecoming when it happened to me many years later, so filled with the shock of recognising a place I'd never seen, that I see my experience on that ship deck as a kind of foretaste of a bigger reality.

Since then I've talked to others who've had a similar reaction to some unfamiliar landscape. The explanation for all of us, I think now, lies not in the past, in childhood or family history, but in the future. I believe that everyone is given this mysterious affinity for some physical *place* as a kind of preview of the true journey home. The place is different for each of us, but the promise is the same – *you have a homeland.* You will not always be a wanderer. There is a place prepared for you, and when you get there you will say, 'I have lived here always.'

The Altarpiece

> [They] acknowledged that they were strangers and exiles on the earth. For people who speak thus make it clear that they are seeking a homeland.

Hebrews 11:13–14 RSV

'Heaven' is the name seekers through the ages have given to this spiritual homeland. For the first thirty-some years of my life, *heaven* and *the Land of Oz* meant much the same to me – fairy-tale places dreamed into being by people whose life in the real world was hard. Very nice for those who could console themselves this way, but not, of course, for rational people.

How I've been drawn – unheedingly, unknowingly, even unwillingly – to a very different view, is the story of this book. Heaven, I believe today, is not only real, but more real than anything else. Real not just in some disembodied post-death existence – though it will continue to be real then too – but real today, right where I am. Heaven, I believe, has only one time.

Now.
And only one place.
Here.

'Place' of course isn't the right word, just the only one we have. A *place* suggests a fixed location where – however distant – I can imagine someday arriving. Above the altar of our church in Mt Kisco, New York, is a painting of the Mount of Transfiguration. Against a sky of gold – in Christian art the symbol of heaven – Jesus holds celestial discourse with Moses and Elijah, while Peter, John and James look on. As these three recall it later, their rabbi's wind-tanned face began to shine with glory, 'and his clothing became dazzling white, far more glorious than any earthly process could ever make it!' (Mark 9:3 TLB).

At that transcendent moment it must have seemed to the three fishermen that their days of homeless wandering were over. After years of trudging the dusty roads behind their footloose leader, hadn't they reached the very courts of heaven? This was it! They'd arrived!

'Shall we put up shelters for you and Moses and Elijah?' Peter asked excitedly. Move in, stay right here?

But of course they hadn't 'arrived' anywhere. Heaven is nowhere that can be fixed on a map. On the Mount of Transfiguration, the journey for Peter, John, and James had just begun.

The Picture Frame

Heaven is nowhere. But it is also everywhere. At any moment the mist may lift and we may find ourselves in that unknown, well-known land. 'So it was *here* I was headed, all along!'

From heaven we can look back and see the changes and chances of our lives as the pathway leading straight to where we stand in joyful wonder. The losses, the seeming detours, the things that most puzzled and distressed us – why, they were the very route by which we came.

And still the way, Jesus' Way, leads on. Away from the mountaintop where we seemed so close to heaven, down into the valley of shadow and struggle. *Why must it be like this?* we wonder. Over the years I've asked hundreds of spiritual pilgrims about the hardest moment of their journey. And for most of them it's been the period immediately following some glorious revelation of God's love.

Why? Why can't we live always in the peace and joy we tasted so briefly? Why should we have to keep stumbling on, forever led away from the heavenly vision?

I believe it's because the heaven to which Jesus the Way is taking us is so very big. From earth we can see so little of that eternal landscape, and he wants to show us so much. 'Don't stand there gazing. You haven't seen anything yet!'

Probably because I have no artistic ability of my own, I love going to museums, letting the perceptiveness of artists show me beauties I would otherwise miss. Some years ago I was at the Johnson Art Museum in Raleigh, North Carolina, when a group of children from a school for the blind was shown through. Curious, I followed along behind. What could these sightless youngsters enjoy in an art gallery?

The sculptures! For this tour, *Don't Touch* rules were suspended; with murmurs of discovery, the children ran sensitive fingers over shapes in marble, steel, wood. One curly-haired little girl, seven or eight years old, was full of questions. 'What's over there?'

'Paintings,' the guide told her.

'What's a painting?'

How, I wondered, *would her guide answer?* Taking the child's hand, the guide led the little girl behind the rope that cordoned off an enormous canvas by Morris Louis. It was a starkly abstract composition: bold streaks of blue, orange, green, against a white background. What could colours mean to this inquisitive young mind? How do you describe 'orange' to someone who's never seen a pumpkin?

As I watched, the guide placed the child's hand on the frame at the bottom of the painting, then slowly led her the length of the picture. At the far end, the youngster gave a nod of satisfaction.

'Big!' she said.

I think often of that scene. I am that child, it seems to me. For a lifetime I've been doing as she did, tracing the lower rim of heaven, guided by the One who sees the picture in all its vivid colour.

'Until you can see,' he tells me, 'I cannot show you what's inside the frame. But if you will take my hand I can bring you close, let you touch the border and learn that heaven is large enough to encompass all that ever happens to you – yesterday, today, tomorrow.'

The past, the present, the future – heaven enfolds them all.

Heaven behind me . . . All the way we walk before we know that the road itself is God. For me this part of the journey lasted more than thirty years. I was given hints of the truth aplenty, but I could not read them. It's only in retrospect that I know that every event of my life was a step on the Way that's been heaven all along.

Heaven around me . . . It's that part of the journey when dimly, wonderingly, always imperfectly, we catch sight of those streets of gold right beneath our feet. It's the strange, contradictory world of grief and joy, despair and hope, where I've lived these last forty years.

Heaven before me . . . This is the landscape where we'll spend longest, and about which we now know least. It's the heaven we'll experience after death, where all we can now be sure of is that Jesus has gone ahead to prepare a place.

Heaven behind, around, before . . . no time or place that is not heaven.

Heaven behind Me

You trace my journeys and my resting places . . . You press upon me behind and before.

Psalm 139

I fled Him, down the nights and down the days;
I fled Him, down the arches of the years;
I fled Him, down the labyrinthine ways
Of my own mind; and in the midst of tears
I hid from Him, and under running laughter. . .
From those strong Feet that followed, followed after.
    But with unhurrying chase,
    And unperturbèd pace,
Deliberate speed, majestic instancy,
    They beat – and a Voice beat
    More instant than the Feet
'All things betray thee, who betrayest Me.'

Francis Thompson – The Hound of Heaven

The Three-Year-Old

Heaven behind me . . . the journey unaware. The trip we understand only in looking back.

In the summer of 1959, John and I travelled with our three children twelve thousand miles by car, collecting story material from Delaware to Texas to Alaska. In those pre-seat belt days, the back of the estate held a mattress where the kids could stretch out. Three-year-old Liz was usually the first to clamber over the backseat and lie down. Scott, aged eight, and Donn, five, would continue a while longer to stare at the passing countryside.

'Wow! Look at that long freight train!'

If the spectacle sounded enticing enough, there'd be a stirring in the back of the car. Slowly disentangling herself from books and teddy bears, Liz would sit up. By then of course, the train or the galloping horse or the drive-in shaped like a giant ice-cream cone would be far behind us.

And from the back of the car would come a small puzzled voice. 'Where?'

I felt the same frustration when, in my mid-twenties, I met my first 'religious' people. They were forever seeing God in the passing scene. 'Wasn't it wonderful how God worked that out!'

Where was this wonder-worker so plainly visible to others? Audible too, apparently. God often 'told' them this or that.

Listening to their matter-of-fact assertions, I felt like a three-year-old in a moving car. Why couldn't I detect these things?

Nor, at age three, did Liz understand the purpose of the long trip. A destination like Independence, Missouri, meant nothing. For Liz, the journey was a series of unrelated events. Some bad – the restaurant where she left her crayon box behind. Some good – the motel with the swimming pool.

Today, looking at the photo album of that summer, Liz can reconstruct the route. Today she knows we went to Independence to interview President Truman. She can see a picture of herself in a yellow dress, standing beside him on a white frame porch.

Charting the early stages of any spiritual journey is a lot like what Liz has to do to make sense of that trip in 1959. Today I know that Jesus is the destination. And because he is also the Way, I know that the goal and the journey are one. With hindsight I can reconstruct the route by which we've come. Line up seemingly unconnected events along the path that is also a Person.

The Pencil Maker

I call it a 'path' because that's how I've come to think of this journey. Not a swift trip on an highway, slicing through mountains and leaping rivers, but a winding trail, intimate, often rough, the route ahead usually obscured by undergrowth. We cannot hurry to heaven; we can only go as fast as our particular landscape allows. The verb *saunter,* Thoreau tells us, comes from the French *sainte terre,* holy ground. It's the pace at which he walked the paths at Walden Pond, the pace a traveller must take along the Way.

For some, the path at least is well marked. I remember Billy Graham's wife, Ruth, telling me once that she couldn't recall a time when she didn't know Jesus.

We were sitting by the wood fire in the eat-in kitchen of the Grahams' rustic home in Montreat, North Carolina, working on a book for children and discussing what concept of heaven a six-year-old would have. The daughter of missionaries, Ruth had grown up in the rural China of the old warlord days, where the Christian community lived in a walled compound. Outside the walls was a world of very visible evil – rich landlords and starving peasants, bribe-taking judges, legal torture, little girls sold into slavery. Within the compound walls, by contrast, were kindness, love, dignity. Microcosms of hell and heaven.

'I had no trouble, at six, picturing either place,' Ruth said. 'Nor understanding that it was Jesus who made the difference.'

The world I grew up in, on the other hand, I told her, revealed no such distinction between godly and ungodly. All the citizens of Scarsdale, New York, to a child's eyes anyway, were equally law-abiding. If some of them went to church, they seemed no different from the rest.

God . . . Jesus . . . heaven . . . such things were never talked about at our house. I remember only one religious discussion with either of my parents all the while I was growing up. The summer I was thirteen I asked my father one day, 'Daddy, do you think there's a God?'

My father, Walter Scott Schindler, was the private detective whose files provided the original Perry Mason stories. A skilled investigator, Daddy, I was sure, would not believe something that wasn't true.

For a moment he didn't answer, reluctant, perhaps, to voice his worldly-wise agnosticism to a thirteen-year-old. At last he took a pencil from his desktop – we were at his office in New York City – and turned it slowly in his hands. 'This pencil,' he said, 'didn't just happen. Someone had to make it.'

He jabbed the pencil toward the window overlooking 44th Street. 'The same way with the world. It wouldn't be here if there hadn't been a – let's call it a Designer, an Architect – to make it.'

I looked down at the street with its stream of Checker cabs headed for Grand Central Station half a block away. From that godlike height, fourteen floors up, I surveyed the hurrying pedestrians, the fretfully honking traffic. What could be the purpose in such a creation? A pencil had an obvious function. But what function had we?

That year, 1941, Europe was convulsed in the most destructive war in history. Night after night I had a recurring nightmare. People would be loading objects onto an airplane – once it was books, another time, tennis balls. In one particularly vivid dream it was hundreds of black patent leather shoes. Then the plane would take off and the people would begin throwing the things out of the window. As they hit the ground, the innocent-seeming objects exploded. I'd hear screams and wake with a scream rising in my throat too.

There was always a moment, just afterward, when a rush of relief would come. *It's only a dream.* And then the full awakening: *It's true! Bombs are falling on people right now!*

I turned away from the office window. *If Daddy was right,* I thought, *and at the beginning there'd been a Designer, he, or it, was certainly no longer around.* If 'God' ever existed, it made no difference now.

It was the only time I ever inquired into my father's beliefs. As for bringing up the subject with Mother . . . religion was 'too personal', the phrase with which she deflected all attempts to invade her inner world.

For me the journey to heaven began without a map.

Eldest Child

> If I find in myself a desire which no experience in this world can satisfy, the most probable explanation is that I was made for another world.
>
> *C. S. Lewis, Mere Christianity*

I was not a happy child.

It's strange how hard that sentence is for me to write. Not that it's untrue. Just that setting it down seems a betrayal of cherished parents.

It's Daddy who would have been most dismayed to read those words. Mother would certainly have disapproved of airing so private a matter. 'I'm sure we all have our troubles, dear. No one wants to hear about someone else's.'

But Daddy . . . Though he died nearly fifty years ago, I can hear his cry of bafflement as though he were reading over my shoulder. Not happy! With a loving family, good health, material blessings beyond anything he dreamed of in his own childhood! He liked to relate how as a boy he'd be sent to the butcher shop, clutching the dime that was to buy meat for a family of nine. 'Don't forget to ask the butcher,' his mother would call after him, 'to throw in the liver for the cat!'

They didn't have a cat.

How could a child as fortunate as me, fail to be happy?

How could I, years later as a young wife and mother, be anything but fulfilled and content? When in 1952 I was diagnosed with clinical depression, Daddy was outraged. 'You have no right to be sad!'

He enumerated the reasons: 'A husband who loves you, beautiful kids, a nice home. And you can have a steak anytime you want one!'

It was all true. That is the terror of depression, the dark mystery I could not explain either to him or to myself. *You can have a steak anytime you want one.* The words have become shorthand for John and me, for all the things that ought to make a difference and don't.

Not that there weren't lots of happy times in my childhood. But as I trace the journey to heaven to its beginnings, a sad-eyed little girl too often looks out from the snapshots.

In her books Catherine Marshall often wrote of the carefree days of childhood. As Catherine's editor for over twenty years, I would often put a question mark by these passages. Even for youngsters less moody than me, I didn't believe childhood was tension free. The specifics of my experience are only variations in our common story.

Like Catherine, I was the oldest of three children – the *responsible eldest.* 'You're in charge now.' In charge of getting the playroom tidied, the dishes dried, my brother and sister ready on time. But Donn, twenty-one months younger than me, and Caroline, two years younger still, were unaware of this hierarchy.

'Daddy and I are counting on you,' Mother would tell me.

'But they don't listen to me!'

'Then set an example. Show them how it should be done.'

Donn and Caroline, however, were not interested in my demonstrations. It's hard to set an example of, say, perfect table setting, when your pupils are outdoors throwing sticks for the dog.

Catherine's parents had counted on her too, she pointed out, and her brother and sister hadn't always cooperated either. 'Why should that have made you feel bad about yourself?'

Why indeed? Where did it come from in me, this sense of not measuring up to some imaginary standard of perfection? What were these failures that loomed so large in my emotions? Though I wasn't good at team sports, I was a competitive swimmer. I was sure I was ugly, but photographs show a child who would have been pretty if she'd smiled.

My sense of worthlessness must have come from some inner source that even now, after many years of psychiatric probing, I don't fully understand. Once, when she was in her eighties, Mother and I were looking through an old photo album. 'We were always so proud of you!' she said. And I thought, *Oh, Mother, why didn't you tell me!*

She didn't, I'm sure, because in the 1930s praise was supposed to make a child conceited. Today's experts disagree. A child's self-confidence develops, in the words of Erik Erikson, under 'the gaze of a delighted other'.

Or perhaps my parents' delighted gaze would have made no difference. Perhaps a low self-image is part of the human condition, common to us all till God's unconditional love shows us a beauty in ourselves beyond all imagining.

The Bereavement

> No noble, well-grown tree
> ever disowned its dark roots,
> for it grows not only upwards
> but downwards as well.
>
> *Carl Jung*

My friend Barbara Gordon framed these words to hang on her living room wall, a reminder that to mount to heaven with Jesus, we must descend into hell with him, too – that personal hell that is different for each of us. That hell where he also went to become our Way.

For me, the time came when my unhappiness could no longer simply be toughed out. I was in my mid-twenties with a husband, two little boys, and a third child on the way – all the good things Daddy pointed out – when the void inside me became immobilizing, driving me to an attic room with a locked door and drawn shades.

Clearly the 'dark roots' of this distress had gone too long unacknowledged. A psychiatrist, Dr Avraam Kazan, guided the uncovering process. Our sessions, three times a week at the beginning, lasted on and off for twenty years. It was Dr Kazan who gave a name to the shapeless sadness I could never shake. He called it *grieving*.

As soon as he said the word, I knew it was the right one. That was what it felt like – some ancient, inconsolable loss. Some immense, inexpressible bereavement. But for whom? 'No one close to me had died,' I said.

'No one had died,' he agreed. 'But at ten months old, you didn't know that.'

The event we were talking about happened long before I could remember. I knew only what I'd picked up over the years from casual references by my parents to a European trip.

Daddy's investigations sometimes took him overseas. The case he was working on in January 1929 involved a counterfeiting ring centred in Paris and would require his staying there several months. It was his long-awaited chance to take Mother, who had never been abroad, along with him. Her parents agreed to come north from Florida to care for me – an ideal arrangement for all concerned.

'Except,' Dr Kazan pointed out, 'for the ten-month-old baby that was you.'

My parents simply disappeared one day, he interpreted my experience, and never, as far as I knew, came back. 'Four months later, when they returned, they would have been strangers. You lost your parents as surely as though they had died in a car crash.' Worse than a car crash for my emotional health, he believed, since the 'bereavement' went unrecognised.

Would this small episode really be enough, I've wondered, to account for lifelong feelings of insufficiency? I think of people I know who suffered actual trauma early in life – whose parents really did die, or who were abused, neglected, abandoned – yet emerged as self-respecting adults. Could a mother and father's absence for just a few months really cast such a long shadow?

Dr Kazan, at any rate, believed it could. 'Babies, you know from having three of your own, are self-centred little creatures. To a baby, especially right around the first birthday when we start becoming aware of ourselves as separate persons, if the mother goes away, it's his fault. The message to the psyche is, *I'm not good enough.*'

Meanwhile, in Europe, Mother had become pregnant again. Ill, unable to keep down the unfamiliar French food, she spent miserable weeks in a hotel room, and a worse week in a rocking berth coming back across the Atlantic. Her parents brought me to the pier in New York to meet the ship. When Mother and Daddy left, I had been crawling. While they were gone I'd not only started to walk but, as Mother recalled, was running up and down the dock, both grandparents in pursuit.

'I looked over the ship's railing and saw you,' she told me once, many years later, 'and I just *groaned.*'

I understood that groan; at the time of this conversation I was chasing my own toddler. And I understood a little more about the melancholy that enveloped me as a child. That groan, the sense of being unwelcome in my world, can still echo in my inward ear like an old cracked record, even today when the music of my soul is very different.

The Portrait

My mother's illness – and no doubt that groan at the demands of an energetic toddler! – continued for the remaining six months of her pregnancy. As for Daddy, he was coping with his own stress. While they were in Paris, a cable from faraway California had informed them of the sudden death of the mother he adored.

I wish I had known Daddy's mother! Her portrait hangs in our living room, a dignified white-haired woman with warm brown eyes behind rimless glasses. I often stop before it, wishing I could talk to her.

'Adored' is too mild a word for the way all seven of her children felt about Isabelle Campbell Schindler. 'She was a saint,' my non-religious father would say. Poor most of her life – she was the one requesting liver 'for the cat' – Daddy remembered her as the most giving person he ever knew, forever bringing a hungry stranger home for a meal or a month of meals. Setting another plate on the table though her own might go empty. Making up another bed even if she had to sleep sitting in a chair.

A reformer, she frequented women's prisons, teaching sewing to the prostitutes who made up the bulk of the inmates. She conceived the idea, radical in turn-of-the-century America, that it was not wantonness that drove these women onto the streets, but hunger. If they were taught a saleable skill, she argued with wardens and police, they would not be forced, on the day they were released, to return to their old trade.

Daddy was devastated by his mother's death. Retracing my journey in those early years, I see my parents coping with their own physical and emotional crises. I see my brother, Donn, born in November 1929, just after the stock market crash. Of financial hardship I was too young to be conscious. But I was very aware that an all-eclipsing newcomer now dominated my small world.

The Loner

> **A man that looks on glass,**
> **On it may stay his eye,**
> **Or, if he pleaseth, through it pass,**
> **And then the heav'n espy.**

> *George Herbert*

If Donn really did get more attention as we grew up, it was simply that the culture of the time placed more importance on boys. My childhood struggles were the common ones of any era – an older child feeling supplanted, one sibling believing another the favourite – which children handle in their various ways.

Mine was to live behind an imaginary door. The bolt was on the inside, to be opened, if at all, to one person at a time. To be one-of-a-group held a nameless terror. Paradoxically, perhaps, I was also a leader – president of the high school drama club, chairman of the war bond drive, editor of the school magazine. Leadership provided a kind of separation.

To maintain my status-apart within the classroom, I carried on for fourteen years a secret competition. This race with only one runner seems so sad to me today that I can hardly bear to look back at it. It began in the third grade, the first one in which test scores were given. If I got the best marks in the class, I would retain my isolation!

From age eight through my last college class at age twenty-two, I ran this self-imposed marathon, no matter how unappealing the terrain. I hated dissecting frogs, I loved reading. But driven by demons I didn't understand, I needed to be best in *every* subject. On the first day of school I'd appraise my classmates, as kids unerringly do. If there was a 'competitor', unaware though he or she was, I'd throw myself into such stupifyingly dull tasks as memorizing chemical tables.

In those war years, students who did well in maths were offered scholarships by technology schools. I remember telling a bewildered MIT recruiter, 'But I *hate* maths!'

Those who run in an earthly race, said St Paul, do it to receive a prize that withers away. To run a phantom race for a prize I didn't want . . . this is the journey without road signs.

I never did find a literal door to hide behind. At home, until I was fourteen, my sister and I shared a bedroom. When I entered high school, my pleas for a room of my own prevailed at last, and Caroline was moved into a small study next door. The study, however, had no closet, while the bedroom had two. It was eminently sensible, the only practical arrangement, for Caroline to keep her clothes where she always had.

To a younger sister, of course, a teenager's room was irresistibly attractive. In and out she would come. A sweater, a hair ribbon. Backwards and forwards: 'I forgot my slippers.' Sometimes when the door opened for the umpteenth time, I would secretly cry.

Once I actually locked the door. When Daddy learned about it, he took the key and hurled it out of the window. He didn't need to tell me I was acting selfishly, 'begrudging your sister one little corner of that big room!' I'd called myself far worse things than selfish. I longed to be a different kind of person, sociable, outgoing.

The strange thing about my distress at Caroline's right-of-access is that she and I were allies in most things. We were, and are, best friends, as close as any sisters I know. That even Caroline could not enter my room without my selfhood being threatened tells me how fragile that self was.

A few years later my yearning for barricades would create tension in my marriage. As for becoming a Christian, when that horizon opened before me, this of course was out of the question. I'd met a number of Christians by then; they were the most mingling, more-the-merrier, wide-open door people I knew . . .

The Goat Woman

In 1987 John and I rented an apartment in Normandy. In the afternoons we'd get in the car and ramble down the country lanes, past cows grazing beneath the region's famous apple trees, turning right or left, headed nowhere in particular.

Within a few miles we'd be thoroughly lost, and empathising with the Allied soldiers who fought their way across this terrain in the weeks after D-Day. Millennia of passing feet and wheels have worn the roadways low, while the woven-hedge fences have built the banks ever higher, so that you travel through sunken green tunnels with never an overall view of the landscape.

It was about 5:00 one afternoon when we passed, scrambling down one of these steep banks through a gap in the hedge, the most extraordinary human being we'd ever seen. She was barefoot, dressed in an assortment of rags that flapped about her almost to the ground, long white hair streaming to her waist.

John braked the car and we looked back, embarrassed to be staring, but wanting to be sure we'd really seen her, so much did she seem a figure of fairy tale. We saw now that she carried a short stick with which she was herding three goats across the lane.

What could give us an excuse to speak to her? 'How about asking directions?' John said. We could tell her – truthfully enough – that we were lost.

The lane was too narrow to turn the car around, so John began backing up. 'I hope this doesn't frighten her away.'

On the contrary, seeing us returning, the goat woman hurried toward us. I rolled down my window to meet a pair of inquisitive brown eyes peering through the wild tangle of her hair.

'Pardonnez-nous, Madame,' I said. 'Please excuse us. We're trying to get home and we're lost.'

I don't know what I expected to hear from this strange individual – medieval Latin if she answered at all!

'Mais non!' she exclaimed in lilting French. 'But no! One is never lost. One cannot be lost! All roads lead to Rome!'

Her lively eyes were darting about the car, front seat, backseat, taking in binoculars, bottled water, the details of our clothes. If we were curious about her, it was clear that she was just as intrigued with us. We'd bought the car in Germany, and she must have seen the *D* on the licence plate.

'You're German! It is good to travel far when one is so young!'

As John was then sixty-four and I, fifty-nine, we liked this view of ourselves. She would have been as glad as we, I think, to keep the conversation going, but the goats had sprinted up the opposite bank. She gave us directions to the nearest town, then clambered after them and disappeared through another break in the hedgerow.

For a moment we stared after her, still not quite believing the encounter. Inside an ungainly body in its fluttering rags was a mind rich with experience and eager as a child's.

One is never lost. All roads lead to Rome!

They did once, of course, in this area, those astonishing paved

28

ways built to carry Roman legions to every corner of the empire. But that evening in 1987, the phrase said something different to me. I heard my own voice: *We're trying to get home and we don't know the way.* Heard the goat woman's answer. *One is never lost.*

What if even the wrong roads we set out on – my childhood need to hide, my neurotic competitiveness – what if even such byways can lead us home in the end? What if all roads lead potentially, not to Rome, but to heaven? Not that any route I choose will take me there, but that nothing can happen to me that Jesus cannot turn into an avenue of grace.

One cannot be lost.

Even the hard roads, the steep, thorny stretches, they too lead home.

> **There let the way appear steps unto heaven,**
> **All that thou sendest me in mercy given.**

When Sarah Flower Adams wrote these lines of her best-loved hymn, 'Nearer My God to Thee', she was ill with the disease that would take her life at age forty-three. Orphaned at five, forced at thirty-two to give up a brilliant acting career because of poor health, she could nevertheless see 'all' that befell her as the pathway to heaven laid by a loving God.

Francis Thompson, too – part of whose wrenching autobiographical poem opens this segment – led a tragic life by any measure. Sick, destitute, addicted to opium, in *The Hound of Heaven* he recounts his self-destructive flight from God. By the end of the painful story he has become 'of all man's clotted clay the dingiest clot'.

Then God speaks. And what God says, at the conclusion of the long poem, is very like what Sarah Adams heard:

> **All which I took from thee, I did but take**
> **Not for thy harms,**
> **But just that thou mightst seek it in My arms.**
> **All which thy child's mistake**
> **Fancies as lost, I have stored for thee at home:**
> **Rise, clasp My hand, and come!**

One cannot be lost.

Packing Barrel

If my parents never talked about religion, there was one family member who did – emphatically, as he did everything. Grandfather Schindler, whose portrait hangs beside Grandmother's in our living room, was a Unitarian minister with a prophet's fire. I remember my brother and me tugging desperately on his arms in a Toronto movie house, trying to get him to stand up for 'God Save the King'.

'I'll not rise for a king!' Grandfather trumpeted in his pulpit-trained voice as everyone turned to stare. 'God save our freedoms and kings be d———d!'

Then in his mid-eighties, he'd retired from the ministry and now worked occasionally for Daddy. 'The world's oldest detective,' said the entry about him in *Ripley's Believe It or Not!* An old man with a white goatee and a shiny bald head, Grandfather could sit in the lobby of a hotel, apparently dozing in a chair, and take in everything that went on. With the invisibility of the elderly and a memory like a tape recorder, he was the perfect undercover agent.

In his own profession of reforming preacher, however, he'd been less successful. Daddy's principal childhood memory, he used to say, was of moving. Grandfather was hopelessly idealistic, hopelessly ahead of his time. If a thing was morally wrong, no matter how central to the local economy, he thundered against it from the pulpit. In Virginia, he preached against tobacco; in Kentucky, against grain alcohol; and everywhere, in the 1880s and nineties, against racial segregation, child labour, and the refusal to give the vote to women.

As one offended congregation after another dismissed their too-visionary minister, Daddy would come home to find his patient mother bent over a packing barrel. Trunks were expensive. Once more she'd be placing books on the bottom, dishes for her family of nine next, then a layer of blankets . . .

She never complained. A move was a chance to extend her prison ministry. 'I have all my young ladies sewing. There'll be others where we're going.'

Undaunted by his failure to sway his flocks, Grandfather continued all his life to voice unwelcome truths. When I first remember him, in the 1930s, he was warning about the military buildup in Germany. My last conversation with him concerned air pollution. It was 1948, a year before his death at age ninety-three, a time when 'environment' to me was still just a word in the dictionary. I'd taken the train out to California to see him, hoping to draw story material from his wealth of memories. Like the time he'd stood by the train tracks in Ohio, a boy of seven, sobbing as Lincoln's funeral train passed by.

But out in Santa Barbara, Grandfather refused to look back. 'Past history! Now if we don't control auto emissions,' he pounded his chair arm for emphasis, 'fifty years from now the air in Los Angeles won't be fit to breathe.'

It was a rigorous religion to which Grandfather introduced me. A passionate stand in God's name against all forms of exploitation and inequality. I never once heard him say the word *Jesus*.

Perhaps exhausted in their youth by so demanding a creed, only one of Grandfather's seven children professed religion as an adult. This was Daddy's sister Helen. A social worker in New York City, Aunt Helen attended the austerely functional red brick Unitarian church on East 35th Street, where I often went with her. In that calm and rational sanctuary, I encountered a moral God I found more satisfactory than Daddy's creator-of-pencils. I was only a visitor at Aunt Helen's church, but whenever I had to fill in a blank under *Religion,* I would write 'Unitarian'.

The Wax-Faced Doll

On a July Sunday in 1995, John and I walked down the hillside from our B&B in England's Lake District, following the church bells to the picture-postcard village of Hawkshead. The sermon in the ancient church that day was on friendship.

The outcome of our spiritual journeys, declared the preacher, Canon Southward, depends in large measure on those who travel with us. He gave as examples two writers, Charles Kingsley and Robert Burns. Asked to explain how he'd maintained his productivity over a long life, Kingsley answered, 'I had a friend.' And Burns, dying of alcoholism at thirty-seven, accounted for his self-destruction in identical words: 'I had a friend.'

'Friends matter!' Dr Southward summed up. They provide guidance, for good or ill, along our path.

A parade of faces rose before me as we climbed back up the hill. Friends who've been good guides, others bad. And some who've been both.

31

One face in particular . . . Because I've come to believe that in every relationship Jesus shows us both something of himself and something about ourselves, I want to draw the portrait of my earliest, most problematic travelling companion. One whose influence was both healing and, I know today, deeply harmful.

I keep it in my dresser drawer – a tiny leather box with a frayed satin lining. Inside the box is an old-fashioned gold locket that opens to display two oval frames. One oval holds the photograph of a handsome woman in her late forties standing beneath the flowering magnolia tree in the yard of our house in Scarsdale. In my nine-year-old handwriting in the facing oval are the words *Pied de Terre.*

The worn leather box, the antique locket, the not-quite-right French, sum up for me the woman in the photo. Her name was Mea Ada Arthuretta Ivimey, and though there were nearly forty years between our ages, she was my closest friend from early childhood until my marriage to John.

Pied de terre – when I took French in school, I discovered the correct phrase is *pied à terre* – was our secret password. Literally 'a foothold on earth', the phrase signified, Mea explained, one's own set-aside space.

The hideaway I sought!

It was our fantasy that when I grew up she and I would have such a place. We spent blissful hours designing it. Sometimes our *pied à terre* was a cottage in a hidden garden, sometimes an apartment in London or Paris, but wherever it was, it was filled with books, cats, and a few – only a few, Mea insisted – exquisite things.

Today I know that we were doing what people have always done when their present life is unsatisfactory: inventing a heaven. How much of Mea's life was lived in imagination I only understood as I grew older. To me as a child, she was simply one of the family, a friend of my parents before I was born, a beloved presence at every Thanksgiving, Christmas, and birthday celebration.

Her own family story, however, was a tragic one. Born in Bristol, England, Mea's sole memory of either parent was of sitting beside her mother on a high four-poster bed, playing with the long auburn hair that spilled across the pillows. Mea, age three, was caressing the silken strands when there was a shriek from the doorway and she was snatched from the room. It was years before she realised that it was her mother's deathbed onto which she had unwittingly climbed.

There was a father in faraway India who died only a few months after his wife. Three-year-old Mea was placed in a Bristol orphanage. There her days were spent in a large grey-walled room lined on three sides with small chests. The chests, one to each child, were for whatever playthings the youngster might have arrived with. Mea's chest was empty. These were the 1890s, when the inequalities of life were not contested.

Mea would watch the other children reach into their chests and draw out a skipping rope, a top, a jack-in-the-box. She'd tiptoe to hers and throw up the lid, trying to make it give up treasures too. This I'm sure is where Mea's skill at make-believe was born. Over the months her empty chest held one imagined delight after another. A doll's house. A Noah's ark. A stuffed dog.

By her fifth birthday the imaginary contents of her chest had taken a single shape. The chest held a doll. A typical sawdust doll of the era, with china hands and feet, golden hair, a red mouth, and blue eyes in a lovely wax face. So firmly did Mea come to believe in her that she was genuinely puzzled each time she lifted the lid and found the doll absent.

Then in 1896, when Mea was six, came amazing news. In far-off America authorities had discovered an uncle who had not suspected Mea's existence any more than she his. He and his wife were on their way to England to take her from the orphanage to a place called New Jersey.

The day came when she was brought to the matron's office to meet her aunt and uncle. She scarcely saw them. Her shy upward glance was stopped by something in her aunt's hand. It was her doll. No mistaking it: sky-blue eyes and flaxen hair, a blue satin dress. Mea reached for the doll without a word. The man and woman from America were strangers. The doll she knew.

On the carriage ride to the hotel where they were to wait for their boat, Mea never took her eyes from it. In the dining room she stabbed her food blindly, afraid to look away lest the doll vanish as it had from the chest. She climbed into the strange bed, clutching the doll tightly, and fell asleep with it pressed to her heart.

In the morning the six-year-old eagerly drew back the blanket. But – what was the horrid thing on the bedspread? There was the pretty dress, the dainty china hands and feet, but where the beautiful face had been, crazily cocked blue eyes stared from a shapeless white mass. The warmth of Mea's body had melted the wax.

She was staring at the ruined doll in grief too deep for tears when her uncle appeared and with a penknife carved a new face in the wax. Mea loved the odd-looking doll for many years. But the story of the child who had held the thing she loved too close was to repeat itself throughout Mea's life. Again and again she crushed love by clutching it, distorting relationships as her needy embrace had once distorted a doll.

The Oak Room

I understood all this only later. All through the 1930s Mea's arrival at our house in Scarsdale meant a party. Mea could put a few teacups and a plate of crackers on the table and make it a banquet: always my mother's best china, linen napkins, and a vase of flowers, even if it was dandelions from the yard.

All her life she yearned for the gracious surroundings she could never afford. In someone else this might have been pathetic, but Mea had the gift of seeing elegance when there was none and making you see it too. She could draw us children into her world of make-believe as fast as you could say let's dress up, and Donn and Caroline and I adored her.

As soon as I could read, she began writing to me once a week in turquoise ink on pearl-grey stationery. In her letters as I grew older, Mea reminisced about her own growing up. The years in New Jersey, though less deprived physically, had been as lonely as those in the Bristol orphanage. The childless couple who brought her to this country lived in an isolated house where curtains were closed because sunlight gave her uncle headaches. Even in a stiffly posed high school picture dated 1906, I could see the large-eyed beauty Mea had become. Her aunt, possibly jealous, banished the teenager to a third-floor room and kept her in her own cast-off black dresses. The love-hungry girl grew into a love-hungry woman.

There were three brief, disastrous marriages, entered into by Mea, I suspect, at the first hint of affection, fled by each man in turn as Mea's need for love proved insatiable. From the first marriage had come a son, Richard. The father vanished at the outset of the pregnancy, and Mea had her baby in the charity ward of a Baltimore hospital.

I met Richard, twenty years older than me, only twice. He was a lifelong alcoholic; I can only imagine the pressure on him to be all that his mother needed. He'd disappear for years on end, then show up needing money. Mea always provided it. She worked over the years as a bookkeeper, a secretary, a store clerk.

It was a wonderful day when I was old enough to take the train into Grand Central in New York, where Mea would be waiting at the top of the ramp. The apartment to which she took me changed through the years, but to each in turn went her few prized possessions. A pair of opera glasses that had been her mother's, odds and ends of china, a 'splendiferous' crystal punch bowl, a teakwood box containing letters, and the gold locket.

The opera glasses and the locket, originally holding miniatures of her parents on their wedding day, had been kept in the safe at the Bristol orphanage until Mea came to America. The portraits of her father and mother had long since been eaten by mildew, and the locket had remained empty until, with Mea's picture in it, it came to me on my ninth birthday

Mea's apartment was not our *pied à terre,* but one detail of our fantasy heaven it did possess. Cats. In every place Mea lived, there'd be an assortment of strays, picked up ill and starving from the city streets and nursed by her to purring sleekness. She kept a supply of flea powders, de-worming pills, eye ointments, ear swabs and grooming brushes. When a stray was too sick to respond to such ministrations, Mea would prepare a delectable meal – cod roe or chicken liver – with a powerful sleeping pill crushed in it, then stroke the ailing animal to its final rest in her lap.

Mea identified with all homeless creatures, and the cats in turn seemed to identify with her. Battle-scarred veterans of many a street fight, at Mea's they comported themselves as ladies and gentlemen, nibbling daintily from Royal Doulton saucers as though they'd never seen the inside of a garbage pail. Her place had that effect on human guests too. In Mea's apartment I was not an eleven-year-old in pigtails and braces, but a refined young woman stirring her tea with a gold-handled spoon.

Mea had one unvarying weekly ritual. For six days she might subsist on cold cereal, eating far less well than her cats. On the seventh day, though, Mea would take the subway in the afternoon to the Plaza Hotel at Fifth Avenue and 59th Street and, at ten past three, step into the dark-panelled Oak Room. Until that hour the room was a men-only lunchtime preserve. But when the room opened to women, Mea would be shown to her favourite corner table.

Her order was always the same: a Manhattan cocktail, a chicken sandwich, and a pot of coffee. And for an hour and a half, in the hush of white linen and attentive service, she would bind up the bruises of the week. The price of that Plaza lunch would have paid for half a dozen nourishing meals at the Automat, but with the money, Mea explained, she was feeding the soul.

Now and then I was invited to join her and had a chance to see the welcome the Oak Room staff gave her. It wasn't that they supposed her to be rich; she made no secret of her circumstances. The Plaza staff treasured her, I think, as I did, for her ability to take common clay and make us see porcelain.

Siren Song

This was the sensitive and sensitising person to whom I poured out my childhood woes, my adolescent insecurities. While my mother recoiled from intimacy, Mea invited it. She was my confidante, my 'Big Sister', as she signed her weekly letter.

From Mea I learned about compassion for wounded things and the uncrushable human spirit. But I also picked up other messages, ones that still whisper in my inmost ear. Mea completely agreed that I was different from other people. Not only different, better . . . finer, more deeply feeling. My brother and sister, while Mea loved them, lacked my 'perception'. My father had a noble spirit, but dealing with crime had dulled it. As for Mother, she was a wholly conventional kind of person – attractive and charming, of course, but utterly incapable of understanding a personality as profound as mine.

These messages were delivered in a thousand ways over the years, not, I'm sure, with the conscious design of alienating me from my parents, but out of Mea's own deep need to be central in someone's life. By my teens I even understood something of her need and the role I'd been assigned in filling it. But I listened anyhow, like sailors in the Greek myth to the siren song luring them onto the fatal rocks. To the self-rejecting young person I was, Mea's words were music indeed.

I listened, and at some deep level I believed. The message could not have taken root unless the soil received it. Belief in a mysterious 'superiority' always grows, I suspect, out of a deep insecurity.

In the inevitable adolescent conflicts with my parents, Mea became the go-between. She alone understood me, she alone could interpret my rarefied thoughts to them. Mother and Daddy may not have grasped my exalted nature, but they perceived only too well the harm Mea's appropriation of me was doing. What bitter confrontations went on among the three of them – once so close – I was never told. I knew only that by the early 1940s Mea came less often to the house in Scarsdale, and finally not at all.

The loss to her was enormous, another in the lifelong pattern of abandonment by those she loved. Her sorrow was so intense that I became even more fiercely loyal, going each Sunday to the corner mailbox with a letter to her, receiving hers at the home of my high school friend Ann Beveridge.

From college I could correspond openly. From Europe in my junior year, I wrote that I'd met a twenty-four-year-old man named John Sherrill who, I was sure, would love her as much as I did. All my letters from Mea went into the teakwood box that is on my desk today. Rereading them now, I'm amazed at the closeness of the relationship between a woman nearing sixty and a teenage girl.

It did not, of course, continue this way, at least on my part. John did indeed enjoy Mea's company when at last they met – her pluck, her gaiety, the aura she could weave around the most ordinary event. With John, though, I was encountering an intimate relationship that did not clutch.

I remember meeting Mea's train at the Chappaqua station near our home north of New York City one day in 1963. John and the children and I had been out of the country for a year; this was her first visit since our return. Stepping off the train, seeing me after an absence, Mea's hands flew up as though to ward off a physical blow.

'Oh!' she cried. 'Don't look so much like your mother!'

She may not have known what she was saying, but I did. I was to have no history, no family, to be solely the creature of her own making. How unconsciously we all do it – define another's identity to fit our need! But by 1963 I'd learned that God's fathering does just the opposite: on the way to heaven we become ourselves.

About Mea's death I will write when I come to consider the heaven that awaits us beyond this life. The rest of her earthly journey is swiftly told. The year John and I married, her granddaughter, Cecily, was born, the child of her son, Richard's, short-lived marriage. Mea befriended his ex-wife and adored the little girl. As

Cecily grew older, I watched the destructive pattern repeat itself. Cecily's mother didn't understand this exceptional child. The girl had refined instincts that Mea must defend against the commonplace influences of her home.

John and I tried in vain to show Mea what she was doing. Cautions were powerless against those love-starved early years. The sad drama was replayed. Mea gripped her granddaughter as she had the wax-faced doll, and forfeited the relationship with both mother and child.

In Chappaqua Mea continued to be a cherished visitor, our three children looking forward to her coming as eagerly as my brother and sister and I had. Then at eighty-four, following a stroke that robbed her of speech, Mea entered Westchester County's home for the aged.

By then our children were grown and married, and writing assignments were keeping John and me on the road. But as often as I could, I would follow the chlorine-scented hallways to the ward where Mea's bed was the second on the left. In warm weather I would wheel her outside, otherwise to a corner of the Day Room, where I would hold her hand and converse for us both.

As one, two, three speechless years passed, I'd find her more and more often asleep. I'd sit by her bed, thinking about her life from orphanage to county home, where from beginning to end for this gallant lady there'd been no *pied à terre*.

I'd think about my journey, too, and the role Mea played in it. I had found Jesus the Way, by this time. In Mea he'd manifested his glad-heartedness and his compassion. But through friends too he reveals those qualities in ourselves that separate us from him. What about my readiness to feel superior to other people?

I had lots of time to ask this question during those silent vigils in the ward, and I received an answer that, for now anyhow, satisfies me. *I was present in Mea's singling out of you,* I believe I heard Jesus say. *When she told you that you were special, exceptional, unique in all the world, it was I who was speaking.*

What I hadn't heard from Mea, he went on, what was missing in the image of him as reflected in her, was that each person on earth was special, exceptional, unique in all the world. *I wish every young girl had a Mea to tell her how much she matters.* To know myself infinitely valued, he told me, is to see into his heart. To judge someone else to be of less value is to miss that heart altogether.

The Glass Partition

If Mea was my closest childhood friend, another has been my closest friend ever since. As the most complex and revealing of all friendships, marriage more than any other shows us God . . . and shows us ourselves. Without John my journey would have been unimaginably different. And it was a literal journey that brought us together.

It was August 16, 1947, the *Queen Elizabeth*'s first night out of New York Harbour. From the deck a few days later I would watch England emerge through the mist, with that strange sense of coming home. But that first night I was mostly absorbed in finding my way around the huge ship.

When the dinner gong sounded, I followed a stream of passengers through a confusion of stairways and corridors to the Tourist Class dining room. A group fare for the passage had been booked by the University of Delaware for thirty-two Geneva-bound students from schools all over the country; in the large room I spotted several tables marked *Delaware Group*. I found a place at one of these and exchanged names with the others sitting there.

My seat happened to face the glass partition through which people entering the dining room could be seen. I was gazing idly at them, couples with children, men in uniform, a group of elderly women, when among the arriving diners I saw a tall, thin, sandy-haired man in his mid-twenties.

That is the man I will marry.

It was too sudden, too certain, to be a thought. It was simply knowledge. A fact, the way the glass partition was a fact, and the slow swaying of the ship. I sat dumfounded. I didn't believe in 'mystic' experiences; they certainly weren't Unitarian and I would have been horrified to think I was having one.

'No!' I told the fact that confronted me. 'Not yet! I can't get married yet – not for a long, long time!'

I supposed – I hadn't really thought about it – that someday I'd get married. But I had so much to do first! I wanted to be a writer. At Northwestern University I'd joined the black students' club, 'the Quibblers', its only white member. I'd brought with me on the boat a thick folder of notes on our as yet unsuccessful efforts to open university housing to blacks. I planned to use the ocean crossing to write a magazine piece about the dismal residences, miles from campus, where blacks were currently shunted. I pictured myself a crusading journalist, a champion of the oppressed like Grandfather in the pulpit and Grandmother in the prisons.

Marriage meant giving up all that. This was the 1940s; all the married women I knew stayed home and 'kept house'.

'No!' I repeated to myself as the tall young man took a seat, of all places, at one of the Delaware tables. 'I don't want to meet him yet!'

Today I believe that marriage to John was part of the Way laid out for me, the Way whose end is Jesus and whose hallmark is surprise.

There was one face among the students at the Delaware tables that I recognised, Jimmy Martin, also from Northwestern. He came over to my table after dinner that first night. 'Let's get up a foursome for bridge,' he said. 'Ask your cabin mate and I'll bring mine.'

And of course the person he brought to the card room half an hour later was the man I wasn't ready to meet.

'John Sherrill, Tib Schindler,' Jim introduced us. 'Why don't you two be partners?'

And so we have been, ever since. Before the ship docked at Southampton, I'd learned that John was from Kentucky, had fought in Italy during the war, and – to my surprise – that he too was an aspiring writer.

We were standing at the ship's railing the night I made this discovery, watching a silver highway of moonlight laid over the sea and talking about what each of us planned to do in Geneva. It was twenty-four hours after our decisive loss at the bridge table to Jimmy and my cabin mate, Lee Soelle. This evening John had suggested dancing, but after stepping three times on my new black pumps, bought for the trip and pinching anyway, he shook his head.

'Guess I'm no better a dancer than a bridge player,' he apologised. 'Let's go out on deck.'

As we shared our writing dreams, I learned that John too intended to buy a bicycle as soon as we got to Geneva. 'I want to get out into the countryside . . .' he said.

'. . . and write about the local people,' I finished the sentence.

For three hours story ideas bounced backwards and forwards between us, while across the dark water the moonlit path seemed to stretch to infinity.

'You know,' John said, 'a man and woman would make an interesting writing team. . . .'

The Last Sunny Day

My *pension* in Geneva was a large third-floor apartment on *rue Charles Bonnet*, home to eight female students from five nations. The landlady, Madame Brulhart, was a tiny, excitable woman who called us 'mes enfants' and rapped briskly on the bathroom door if the tub water ran too long.

John's *pension* was half a mile away on *rue Calvin*. We'd been told that Geneva in the autumn would be rainy, but the sun was out when he parked his bicycle outside Mme Brulhart's one Tuesday morning shortly after university classes began.

'This may be the last sunny day,' he said. 'We can make up European History, but we might not have another chance to bike out and meet the country people.'

We missed a lot of European History that September, as one cloudless day followed another, but we got to know Alpine villages, ruined castles, and each other. 'It's the last sunny day!' John would call up to my window as he balanced his bike at the kerb. And we would set out, with a baguette of bread, a wedge of Gruyère cheese, and a pad of paper. We talked to dairymen and pig farmers, cheese makers and wood-carvers. I was exploring a new country, a new culture – and for me something even newer. I was discovering what it was to wake in the morning and fall asleep at night with a single person on my mind.

Years later, reading about Christ-centred lives, I understood how someone could 'pray without ceasing'. It wasn't a question of effort. They were in love; they couldn't help themselves.

It was on one of our outings toward the end of September, as we gathered up the leftovers of our picnic, that John, looking thoughtful, said, 'We really should get married *before* Christmas.'

I stopped packing my bike basket and stared at him. Marriage had never even been mentioned. Certainly I'd never told him about that strange 'knowing' on the *Queen Elizabeth*.

'There's a three-week break then,' John went on, as though the matter was long decided. 'We could go down to Italy, write about how things have changed since the war. But we'd need to be married.'

It was true; in the Europe of 1947, 'decent' single women did not travel with male companions. The story idea – a soldier revisiting battle scenes – was a good one too. Ideas bubbled up from both of us. The fact that we would marry was as obvious, now that it had been said, as useless to debate, as the snowcapped Alps soaring above us. And as hard to accomplish, we were to learn, as to climb those distant peaks.

I learned something that day about the ideas we reject offhand. The prospect that had seemed so forbidding in theory, marriage-in-the-abstract, vanished like the phantom it was in the face of a specific relationship. There is no marriage-in-general, only marriages, each different. Conflicts there would certainly be in ours, as in every close relationship, but not the home versus career tension I'd imagined.

Having learned this about marriage, how was it that I held on so long to another stereotype, Christians-in-general? *They,* I believed, were all the same. Why was I so slow to grasp that there are no 'Christians-in-the-abstract', only the specific relationship of each believer to Jesus?

The Letter

Having settled that we should marry before Christmas, a question arose as we pedalled down the mountainside that day. How would our two sets of parents feel about this? We'd known each other exactly six weeks. Wouldn't both families, reasonably, want us to wait awhile?

'We'll write to them,' John said. 'Explain the travel situation.'

And so our first completed joint writing project turned out to be a letter. They were bulky envelopes by the time we sealed them – one addressed to the Sherrills in Louisville, one to the Schindlers in Scarsdale. Inside each one were twelve pages, six written by John, six by me, covering what we believed was any conceivable question a parent could ask. They were prodigies of polished prose, written and rewritten on our typewriters, then copied out by hand.

Together we biked to the *Bureau de Poste* and stood hand in hand at the window grille as the two momentous envelopes were weighed, stamped, postmarked '3 *Octobre* 1947', and whisked from view. Nothing to do now but wait for our families' reactions to so much good news.

It was only on our return to the States a year later that we heard the drama of the envelopes' arrival. It had never occurred to us that mail from Europe reached New York a day sooner than it got to Kentucky . . .

My mother was surprised one noontime, she related, when she opened the envelope with the Swiss stamps, to see unfamiliar handwriting on half the pages. The water in which she was hard-boiling eggs burned away as she stood in the front hallway reading. She smelled the scorching pot, snatched it from the stove, and telephoned my father in the city.

It took Daddy only ten minutes to cross the street to Grand Central and catch the 12:46 to Scarsdale, where Mother met him at the station. He read the letter as she drove home, went to the phone without taking off his coat, and got the information operator in Louisville.

'Wait till this evening,' Mother urged as he wrote down the Sherrills' number. 'You're upset now and I'm sure they are too. Why, Mr Sherrill's probably at work. Let's give us all a few hours to think about this.'

'I can't think about something I know nothing about.' He tossed the letter on the sideboard and mixed a rare midday Old Fashioned. 'You say his father's at work – what kind of work? We know nothing about these people in Louisville. There are precious few facts in all those pages.'

And so there were, I know today, rereading them. Not the kind of facts parents want. They were *our* facts – ecstatic descriptions of one another's looks, talents, brilliance. Glowing plans for our future as travel writers.

Daddy's agitation, Mother knew, came in part from the hard lessons of his profession. A large part of his practice involved not headline-grabbing murder cases, but behind-the-scenes marital inquiries. Parents dubious about the 'count' a daughter had met in some foreign country. Wires would crisscross the ocean between the Schindler Agency and affiliates in France or Spain or England until the identification was complete: *The Comte de Merveau, aka Sir Neville Burne-Williams, is one Henry Bates, born 1903 in Milltown, Kansas, wanted in Indiana on five counts of desertion and bigamy.*

Perhaps it was this that made Daddy's tone more confrontational than cordial when the two families met over the phone that evening. The conversation, as recalled by the four participants, went like this:

'This is Walter Schindler in New York. I want to speak to Lewis Sherrill.'

'This is Lewis Sherrill.'

'Mr Sherrill, I understand that your son wants to marry my daughter.'

A very, very long silence from Louisville. Then: 'I believe you are under a misapprehension, sir. My son is in Geneva, Switzerland.'

'So's my daughter.'

And after we'd laboured so hard over the letter, this is how John's parents got the news. Daddy's interrogation continued. 'What line of work are you in, Mr Sherrill?'

'I'm dean of the Presbyterian Seminary here. May I ask, sir, what your work is?'

'I'm a private eye.'

When the mothers' turn came – few households in 1947 had more than one telephone – the talk was on a more personal level. The gentle southern voice from Louisville, my mother recalled, seemed to be summoning courage to ask a particular question. At last it came out.

'Are you, um . . .' John's mother faltered, 'that is . . . you and your husband, do you . . . are you Christians?'

'Why, of course!' said my mother, to whom 'Christian' meant someone who donated clothes to the Salvation Army.

And four very relieved parents went to bed that night.

The relationship between our two fathers, which began so inauspiciously, turned out to be one of life's happy ironies. Two weeks after that phone call, the Sherrills travelled to New York to meet my family. Before long a deep friendship grew between the two men – the scholarly theologian with an alphabet of advanced degrees after his name, and the self-educated and agnostic New Yorker. It would be Lewis Sherrill, seven years later, who would officiate at Daddy's funeral.

It's the question John's mother asked during that telephone conversation, though, that tells me about the people John and I were in 1947. Even if our letter had reached Louisville before the call came from New York, she would have had to ask it. In the introductions that we thought covered everything that mattered, we'd never thought to mention religion.

The High-Ceilinged Room

Civil marriages, we were told, were performed at the *Mairie*, Geneva's city hall. One afternoon the second week in October, we stowed our bikes in the rack outside that pinnacled structure and found our way to the marriage licence bureau on the second floor.

It was our first encounter with Swiss bureaucracy. We progressed through a labyrinth of offices till we found ourselves standing at a counter filling out a five-page form. This document turned out to be merely a request for permission to fill out the *real* form, which we could pick up in another office by presenting a stamped authorisation issued at still a third location.

So it went, visit after return visit. Forms in duplicate, forms in triplicate, forms requiring witnesses, forms requiring fees. And at each outpost of this mysterious paper kingdom, a long line of patient Swiss who'd no doubt been standing in such lines since they could write their own names *(all caps, black ink)*.

Again and again we pedalled to the *Mairie*. We brought financial statements. Medical reports. An affidavit to our identities from the American Consulate. On an afternoon off from paperwork, we went to a jeweller and chose two slender gold bands. But now a technicality appeared for which there seemed no solution. Under Swiss law, when a woman under twenty-one wished to marry, it was her parents who had to apply for the licence. 'And as Mademoiselle is only nineteen . . .'

In the largest, highest-ceilinged, darkest-panelled room of the *Mairie* that John and I had yet entered, sat a very small, very senior official. Gravely he thumbed through the by-now sizable sheaf of papers on the matter of M Sherrill and Mlle Schindler. The very senior man was very sorry. Since my parents had not come forward to make the necessary application . . .

Licence Denied.

On the radio a few years later, I heard a sermon about Judgement Day. 'Narrow is the way which leadeth unto life!' the preacher thundered. I'd never heard that verse from the Gospel of Matthew – or much else from the Bible. But as the minister enumerated the requirements for admission to heaven, I nodded. Squarely in front of the gates of Paradise stood the *Mairie* of Geneva.

The Porch of the Church

It was mid-November before we worked our way back up the rungs of authority to that high-ceilinged room. By then John and I had known each other three months, and for half that time had been pursuing authorisation to marry. What if, we pleaded with the senior official, we were to provide written permission from my parents?

'An affidavit,' John added in a stroke of insight into Swiss mentality.

'Legally documented,' I picked up on it.

'Duly notarised,' said John.

At *affidavit* the official looked up, at *documented* he nodded, at *notarised* he actually smiled. It was possible . . . with the proper papers, properly certified . . .

We cabled a plea to New York for a notarised statement approving the marriage, and in a week's time it arrived at Mme Brulhart's *pension:* my parents' signatures and a notary's above an elaborate embossed seal that, we were sure, would satisfy the most bureaucratic eye.

It did not.

The official scanned it, shaking his head. It was too . . . it just didn't . . . 'Look! The wife's signature is above the husband's. That's wrong to start with.' There was only one document where there ought to be two. And so on.

We were as downcast pushing our bikes back up the hill as we'd been elated rolling down. From our separate *pensions* we wrote my parents twin descriptions of the latest rejection. We must have caught the flavour of fussy Swiss officialdom, because a week after our letters reached New York, two truly spectacular documents arrived on *rue Charles Bonnet.*

They were notarised statements worded the same as before, but this time on thick, cream-coloured, legal-length paper encased in glassine and bound in royal blue folders. In addition to the crimp-seal of the notary, the sheets had a lower border made up of that postwar American novelty, grocery store savings stamps. Along the top was a row of eagles from my brother's ink-pad set, on the outside of the folders, the shield-shaped seal of The Schindler Bureau of Investigation.

My sister had added the clinching detail. A woman's signature, we'd written, carried little weight in Swiss law. Swiss women could not even vote – nor, as Mme Brulhart said, would a decent woman want to. To the sheet with Daddy's signature, therefore, Caroline had glued her treasured second-prize red ribbon from the local cat show.

It was these works of art that we carried to the *Mairie* the next day. We worried, in fact, that my fun-loving family had made too much of a game of it. But not even a suspicion of humour, apparently, brightened those solemn precincts. At the sight of the documents the senior official beamed. Now *these* were properly executed papers! We caught a certain wistfulness in his voice and feared for future applicants.

Two days later we were issued a marriage licence.

One more legality remained. In that Calvinist canton, where church and state functioned as one, a marriage licence merely allowed a couple to 'post their banns' – to attach to the door of their local church a declaration of their intention to marry. The banns had to remain in place three weeks, during which time anyone with grounds to oppose the marriage was to come forward. It was November 28 when our banns were put up at the entrance to the church nearest *rue Charles Bonnet*, a grey stone structure with an elaborate wooden porch.

There the precious document flapped in the snow squalls of Geneva's approaching winter, a small sheet of paper tacked to the church door with a dozen others: our names, birth dates, and other statistics. For 'home parish' we'd given the names of our home towns, but when it came to 'date of baptism' we'd been stumped. John was pretty sure he'd been baptised and I was pretty sure I hadn't been; under the impatient eye of the registrar-of-church-documents we'd blurted out random dates in our birth years.

Banns, the registrar assured us, were seldom challenged, certainly not in the case of foreigners nobody in the city knew. At last we could set our wedding date: Saturday, December 20, the day after the university closed for the Christmas holidays.

On the way to the tram for classes – there was too much snow now to bike – I'd step up to the church door and read our names. The name of the church I never learned. Nor did it even once occur to me to open that door and go inside.

The Travel Writers

December 20 dawned sunny and cold after an all-night snowstorm. We had asked Mme Brulhart and her counterpart at John's *pension*, Mme de Marignac, to serve as our witnesses. After a honeymoon in Switzerland – it was too late to get an Italian visa in my married name – I'd be moving into John's room at 9 *rue Calvin*.

We'd moved my steamer trunk there the day before. The de Marignacs were a proud old Geneva family reduced to renting out rooms to paying guests. Their austere townhouse was in the very shadow of sombre St Peter's Church, from whose pulpit in the 1500s John Calvin preached his stringent reforms.

We'd written our families that the marriage was set for 10:00 a.m., a more seemly sounding hour than our actual appointment at the *Mairie*, 9:50.

For days Mme Brulhart had been in a lather of excitement. On the twentieth, she woke the entire household at 5:30 and provided a stand-up breakfast. When I'd put on my dark blue suit and rechecked the suitcase packed for the honeymoon, there were over two hours to wait.

Through the front window at 8:45, I saw John making his way over the snow drifts, a bouquet of miniature white carnations in his mittened hand. We set out for the tram stop, Mme Brulhart marching erectly between us to remind us that we still faced an hour of celibacy. White-haired, patrician Mme de Marignac joined us outside the marriage clerk's office on the third floor. The 9:40 couple emerged, and the four of us filed in.

At a desk beneath a huge wooden wall clock sat a grey-bearded man in gold-rimmed spectacles. John and I took two straight-backed chairs across from him, our witnesses on either side of us. Without preamble the man began to read aloud from the form in his hands. The husband was to control all finances, make all decisions, have sole say over the upbringing of children. *The husband will choose the conjugal residence . . . The church affiliation of the husband will constitute the church membership of his dependants . . .*

I wondered if Mme Brulhart and Mme de Marignac, sitting stiffly to our left and right, were recalling the same words read long ago to them – and lived out day by day, I suspected, in their marriages. I clutched my carnations, answered 'Oui, monsieur' to a number of questions, and signed my name – below John's – to the marriage certificate. At 9:56 on the clock above him, the bearded officiant rose and held out his hand.

'Puis-je etre le premier de vous feliciter, Madame.' May I be the first to wish you well, Madame.

At 'Madame' I glanced automatically right and left, but neither Mme Brulhart nor Mme de Marignac moved to take the outstretched hand. And with a start I realised that 'Madame' was me. The four of us left the room as the 10:00 wedding party entered. Going down the stairs, John and I paused on the second-floor landing and put a ring on each other's finger.

In the wording of the marriage certificate, and certainly in the eyes of our two landladies, this ceremony was a preliminary only, a mere legality prior to the real marriage, which must take place in church. 'We'll have a church wedding when we get home,' we assured the two women, untruthfully.

Since October we'd been setting francs aside for our wedding trip. In Bern, the Swiss capital, two hours by train from Geneva, we checked into the ornate *Bellevue*. We were back in Geneva the next day. In the real, non-student world, the hoarded cash had lasted less than twenty-four hours. 'We'll have a church wedding in the States,' we repeated to Mme de Marignac as she unlocked the door to our room. Her stern-lipped silence told us she doubted such an ecclesiastic event would ever take place – and in fifty-four years it never has.

If someone had asked me that day, as I put my things into the dresser drawers John had emptied for me, what the years ahead held for us, I would have answered without hesitation, 'Travel writing!' Though my exposé of racism at Northwestern had been turned down everywhere I sent it, we'd already sold a tongue-in-cheek description of Swiss customs inspection to the *Louisville Courier Journal*. We could look forward, we believed, to a lifetime of exploring new places.

How very accurate this forecast was to prove, I didn't know – nor how utterly unlike what I expected. Travel John and I have certainly had, but the real journey has been the interior one. The truly new places we've visited have not been in South America or Africa or Asia, but along the road to heaven.

The Welcome

I had a foretaste of what our reception in that ultimate destination may be when John and I returned to the States in the autumn of 1948.

I'd written to my parents that John had grown a beard. It was very full and very red, and it seemed only fair, at a time when beards were a rarity in America, to prepare them. Daddy wrote back that we weren't to worry; he'd arranged for the Coast Guard to take John off the *Mauretania* out at sea and bring him ashore after dark. I was used to Daddy's brand of humour; John was not. Two hours before we docked he disappeared into the men's shower room. He emerged clean shaven, the upper half of his face deeply tanned from weeks spent biking through Italy that summer, his jaw and chin a sickbed white.

My parents, sister, and brother, waiting on the pier, took this two-toned apparition to their hearts anyway. And when the cat climbed into his lap that evening, his approval was official.

It was my welcome into his family, though, that I remember best. John's sister, Mary, had written me several times in Geneva. Now another warm note from her was waiting to greet me in Louisville – Mary and her husband, a lieutenant commander in the navy, lived in Norfolk, Virginia. John's parents held a reception for us there in Louisville, where some of the guests, I thought, looked a little dubiously at this northerner the Dean's son had thrust upon them. Never, however, did Mother and Dad Sherrill make me feel an outsider. My ignorance of their world of church and seminary, my total lack of domestic skills – the sewing, cooking, entertaining at which John's mother excelled – must have alarmed them. But they embraced me from the start as a second daughter.

I know today that this grafting of me into another family was a preview of an even more tremendous inclusion – the believer's welcome into the family of God. And inherent in this hint of things to come was the fact that Dad Sherrill was blind.

John had told me about being summoned to camp headquarters during his basic training in Texas, six years earlier, to learn that his father's eyesight was failing. From Camp Wolters he'd been granted a week's 'compassionate leave' to allow his father to see him a final time.

I'd wondered how a blind man could continue teaching, but Dad's scholarship never slacked. I would come upon him in an unlit room, his fingers tracing the lines on a big Braille page. Because he believed his blindness would be a distraction in the lecture hall, he would stand at the lectern turning the pages of a book he couldn't see, calling on his exceptional memory for long verbatim passages. Once when I'd written an article about him, I received an irate letter from a seminarian who'd studied under Dad in the early 1950s, accusing me of lying about the blindness.

Certainly he seemed to see. He never failed to say something complimentary about my appearance. 'You're looking so pretty today!' Or, 'What a lovely outfit!'

Even now I have trouble believing that Dad never saw me. He *did* see me, an inner voice insists. He saw me and I was beautiful! And of course in a sense he did see me – looked at me through the lens of his love. Saw as we're seen in heaven. Saw the beauty of his own spirit and accounted it mine.

The Bridge

When John and I returned to Europe in 1949, we carried letters from half a dozen editors expressing interest in articles on the post-war recovery there. We found a one-room apartment on Paris's Left Bank. And it was in that city that I had another of these intimations of heaven, the significance of which I would only understand later.

On January 1, 1950, the rent on our room had doubled. We'd just mailed the last of a series of pieces on the black market in various countries. Perhaps it was time to go home? On the tenth, payment for the series arrived, enough for two off-season boat fares back to the States. Bundling up against the cold, we set out on foot for the Cunard-White Star ticket office on the Right Bank.

It was on the bridge crossing the Seine that the experience occurred. In the middle of the *Pont Neuf,* I suddenly knew that 'home' wasn't Scarsdale, New York, or Louisville, Kentucky.

We *were* home.

This was a very different phenomenon from that vivid sense of 'homecoming' on the deck of the *Queen Elizabeth* three years earlier. That had been an inward experience – today I'd call it a spiritual one – a mysterious 'belonging' that I couldn't account for.

But in Paris we did belong. We loved it here! Living was cheap, we knew lots of people, to John's delight, and I had lots of museums to go to. I was studying Egyptian art at the School of the Louvre, and as long as John was enrolled at the Sorbonne, the G.I. Bill covered most living expenses. Europe provided endless story material. We'd meet after classes in the little park at the foot of the *Tour St Jacques* and, over a lunch of salami and crusty bread, plan the next material-gathering trip from this rail hub of the continent. Paris was the obvious place to settle for good.

And with this realisation, the world in my head reassembled itself. Like all American schoolkids in the 1930s and forties, I'd grown up gazing at a Mercator Projection wall map of the world: the United States at the centre, symmetrically framed by oceans, Europe off on the right, Asia on the left. Now I felt geography come apart, slide, and shift like the ice breaking up on the river beneath us.

When the motion stopped, Paris was at the centre. I felt the vast Eurasian continent stretching eastward thousands of miles to the Pacific. Saw America somewhat as I'd always thought of Australia, far away across an endless expanse of sea. I felt the ache of those many-times-great-grandparents when the sons and daughters who were my ancestors left the farms and villages that had been home time out of mind.

All this just crossing a bridge.

'Can we walk a little faster?' John said. 'My ears are freezing.'

We strode briskly along the *rue de Rivoli* while I wondered how to explain that, suddenly, I didn't want a berth on a boat. The ticket office was just ahead. But now it was John who slowed his pace.

'Honey,' he said, stopping in the middle of the pavement, 'I don't know how to put this. I know you want to go home, and I thought I did too. But just on the way here, all at once I knew – this *is* home.'

This is the way perspective changes, the saints tell us, when we make heaven our homeland. What was central moves to the edges, while something that was only a name becomes the place from which we measure every distance.

The Dragon's Lair

> **The journey to heaven leads past the place where the dragons lie.**
>
> *Cyril of Jerusalem, 315?–386*

As it turned out, the decision to make Paris our home base was swiftly overrulled by an 'impossible' pregnancy.

We'd scoured the newspapers till we found a cheaper apartment. In a single taxi trip we moved our possessions: two suitcases, two typewriters, a cardboard box of books, and another holding dishes, hot plate, and skillet.

The new place was a sixth-floor walk-up just off the *rue St Jacques:* two tiny sky-lit rooms beneath a slanting roof on which John regularly bumped his head. The five lower floors were mostly occupied by Arab families. Floor by floor, as we circled up the stairs, we'd breathe in aromas of lamb and spice.

Our own meals we ate most of the time in a state-subsidised students' restaurant in the next block, where the eye of the cockerel head might stare balefully from the bottom of the soup bowl. We loved Near Eastern food, though, and would sometimes splurge on dinner at a Moroccan place. Why, then, did the hallway odours in our building make me feel so strange? Queasy . . . More than once I reached the communal bathroom on the fourth floor barely in time to be sick to my stomach.

By the middle of March, I didn't even have to smell food to feel the waves of nausea begin. Climbing the stairs one afternoon, I had to lean against a wall till the dizziness passed. One of our neighbours, a large, cheerful Algerian woman who always called 'Bonjour!' through her open door, came out and led me into her living room. Shooing cats and children off the sofa, she made me lie down.

'It's this way with me, too,' she said, 'the first few months. Especially when it's a boy. Boys are always more trouble.'

The first months? When it's a . . . Was I . . . ?

I couldn't be! The gynaecologist I'd seen in Geneva before we married had told me I could not conceive without surgery. Since newspapers of the day were full of Russia's latest 'Five Year Plan', John and I had decided on a five-year plan of our own. That long to launch our writing careers, then the operation and hopes for a family.

But at the end of March, as telltale signs persisted, I visited an obstetrician. On a day of squally rain, both John and I returned to the doctor's office to be told that the impossible had happened. But the baby, the physician went on, had no chance of survival. 'Continuing the pregnancy threatens Madame's life too,' he said as he filled out the admission form for the hospital where I could get the abortion.

We sat numbly in our apartment that night, listening to the rain on the sloping roof. The excitement we'd felt at the prospect of being parents had turned to confusion, which we confided in letters to our families that night.

My father wrote back at once. In typical take-charge fashion he'd already lined up 'the best obstetrician in New York'. Return boat fare for two was enclosed. So once again we made that walk across the Seine to the Cunard-White Star office.

It was in the fourth century that a father of the church wrote of the dragons on the way to heaven. That's how we know we're on the true route, Cyril of Jerusalem advised his congregations: A dragon will roar from its hiding place only if it's being threatened.

My own dragons lay not in the life of a writer in Paris, but back in New York. In 1950 I knew nothing about dragons, still less about heaven. But I was on that journey nonetheless, as each of us is, knowingly or not. I know today that had we made our permanent home overseas as we intended, I would not have encountered those dragons that each of us must face. Not so soon. Perhaps not ever.

Or perhaps the One who designed us for heaven would have planted my particular dragons in another place under another guise. Perhaps there is no place we can hide where his love will not confront us with the creatures of our darkness. I only know that France was for me, and still is, a place without shadows, a place of perpetual studenthood, where I can learn and learn without ever having to graduate into the world of application. To go forward, I had first to go back.

The Water Bottle

At the end of April, John and I left Paris for Cherbourg to board the very ship on which we'd met. Because the port was still choked with wartime wreckage, the *Queen Elizabeth* was anchored offshore. From the pier a gangplank led down to a launch that ferried passengers to the ship.

It was a breezeless morning, the gentle swell of the water imperceptible to the eye. Yet as my foot touched the deck of the launch, my stomach rose into my throat. I dashed for the railing and was violently sick. All the way out to the *Queen* I leaned wretchedly over the side. 'It will be better on the ship,' John kept saying.

It wasn't better. We found a couch where I lay down while he got our cabin assignment. Then he helped me down to C Deck and into the stateroom's lower bunk. And there I lay for the five-and-a-half-day crossing. We'd looked forward to a sentimental revisiting of the lounge where we'd met over a bridge table, the deck where we'd first talked about writing. But nothing could have been less romantic than this trip! Even to turn my head on the pillow brought waves of nausea.

The ship's doctor came several times to urge me to swallow some water, but the tiniest sip brought on the terrible dry retching from an empty stomach. 'Pregnant women should not sail,' the doctor lectured, as if I could disembark in mid-ocean.

As bad luck would have it, the crossing that spring was unusually rough, setting some kind of record for broken bones and dishes. At one dinner seating John, an unforgivably good sailor, was the only passenger in that huge Third Class dining room.

'I had two helpings of salmon and two . . .'

'Stop!' I managed to rasp before a fresh spasm gripped me.

Several times a day, as the doctor had instructed, John would hold a moist towel to my lips. The rest of the time I lay staring at the bottom of the upper bunk, understanding as never before my mother's misery, pregnant with my brother, making this same trip twenty-one years earlier.

Dehydration brought on a strange delirium. On the top shelf of the refrigerator in Scarsdale, Mother kept a bottle of ice water, a narrow glass jar with ridged sides and a red metal cap. Water would bead on the outside and run in little rivulets down the ridges. I could see that bottle, two feet away. . . Again and again, in the closest thing to a hallucination I've ever experienced, I reached for it, ran my fingers down the cool moist glass, unscrewed the red cap, lifted it to my lips . . .

Daddy was on the pier as John led me, ill and wobbly, down the gangplank. 'As soon as the doctor gives the go-ahead, young lady,' he announced, 'I'm taking you down to Florida to get some sun.'

Mother was already down at her parents' home in Miami Beach, he explained. Both John and I were grateful, at that point, for Daddy's authoritative ways. John's priority was finding a job to pay the upcoming doctor's bills, and I was incapable of thinking so much as an hour ahead. It was days before the ground stopped rising and falling beneath me. No wonder my seasick mother had groaned at the sight of an active toddler!

As promised, Daddy had secured an appointment with a leading obstetrician. Leaving John in the waiting room of Dr Locke MacKenzie, I was passed from nurse to nurse, disrobed, gowned, and introduced to a dignified man with grey-streaked hair who performed a swift examination. A few minutes later in his consulting room, Dr MacKenzie gave a nine-syllable name to the anatomical problem that had brought us back to the States.

'Nothing to be alarmed about. No reason why you won't have a perfectly healthy baby.'

He handed back the letter I'd brought from the Paris doctor. 'Frenchmen tend to be hysterical. Your father says he'd like to take you to Florida. That's fine. I'll need to see you in a month.'

Dr MacKenzie had risen and was holding out his hand. I suppose I shook it, but since the words 'healthy baby', I'd wanted only to rush to the waiting room with the news. John and I walked down Park Avenue two feet above the pavement. We were going to be parents! With the Paris doctor's bleak prognosis, we hadn't allowed ourselves to think past the pregnancy.

'Early October,' John repeated the due date. 'We should probably wait a month or two after that, don't you think, before heading back overseas?'

I agreed. I knew nothing about babies, but it made sense to wait a few weeks before travelling with one. That an infant would in any way alter our lifestyle did not occur to us. How much room could someone that small take up? Maybe back in Paris we'd want to find accommodation with a bathroom on the same floor, John acknowledged. And maybe not so high up in the building, I added, thinking of six steep flights carrying . . . whatever it was babies needed. Cradles, nappy pails, bottles – we were innocent of such things. To us a baby was a miniature person with correspondingly miniature needs.

The Door

And while we blithely planned our future in Europe, closer at hand the dragons lay in wait. The first one to creep from its cavern in the unconscious was the old wish to barricade myself from the world.

In Florida one night I had an excited phone call from John to say he'd found a furnished apartment on Manhattan's upper West Side, only a short bus ride from Columbia University where I'd enrolled for the summer semester to complete my college degree.

The apartment, he went on enthusiastically, was the entire top floor of a private home. Access was through the family's living quarters on the lower floors, but the landlady, Mrs Connors, had assured him they would not be disturbed by our comings and goings. 'She's awfully nice – says she'll put milk and eggs in the refrigerator the day I move in.'

Though the decor, he added, was not what we would have chosen, running to fringed lampshades and pastel prints of Jesus, the rooms were large and sunny. We had a living room, a dining room, a kitchen, two bedrooms. When Mrs Connors learned I'd be going to school, she'd had her husband and son carry a desk upstairs.

I returned to New York in early June. 'If you give me your grocery list,' our obliging landlady offered, 'I can pick up things for you while I'm out.'

The list I gave her grew shorter each week, as she kept our larder supplied from downstairs. Several times a day there'd be a cheery 'Yoo-hoo!' from the stairwell. 'I baked an extra loaf of bread while I was at it,' or 'It was just as easy to double this casserole recipe.'

When she discovered I was pregnant, Mrs Connors' solicitude redoubled. Her own daughter and grandchildren, to her grief, lived in far-off Minneapolis. Now the good Lord, whom she seemed to know very well, had sent me in her place. She had a crib in the basement – the good Lord had told her not to throw it out – that her husband would bring up when the time came. She'd been loaning me her vacuum cleaner; now she insisted on doing our cleaning.

It was, to all appearances, the perfect apartment. Unlike the one in Paris, it had walk-in closets, its own large bathroom, abundant hot water.

What it did not have was a door.

Nothing to define where the Connors' space ended and ours began. A door might not have discouraged our benefactress; she could have knocked as well as yoo-hooed. But before long that missing door loomed in my mind till it was bigger than all the place's pluses.

Meanwhile John had a more serious problem to deal with. Two large New York newspapers had recently gone out of business; longtime journalists were taking jobs as typists and proofreaders.

On his feet all day job hunting, one more out-of-work writer in a market glutted with them, John had more on his mind than my inability to accept the friendly overtures of our landlady.

'I was just lucky to find this place,' he'd remind me. Housing of any kind in Manhattan was hard to come by; something this size for what we could afford with an occasional article sale was unheard of. 'If you'd just go half-way to meet her – ask her up for coffee now and then.'

But it wasn't now and then, it was all day long. Both John and I were still writing three hours a day, John at night and I, theoretically, after school. As long as my typewriter clacked away, Mrs Connors stayed downstairs. But a moment's silence drew her like a magnet.

I took to going to a luncheonette after classes at Columbia, working there on a yellow pad until the waitress asked the third time if I was going to have anything else. I sat on a bench on the concrete island in the middle of Broadway, watching the house till I saw Mrs Connors go out. Why was it so impossible for me to accept her well-meant attention? Still suffering bouts of nausea, I should have been delighted to have so caring a neighbour.

Impossible for me, however, it was. The root of my need for private space was too old, too inaccessible to logic. Week after week I enumerated to myself all the advantages of that apartment. As I had since childhood, I condemned myself as selfish. Antisocial. I'd never cried a lot, but I did now, at almost every yoo-hoo from the stairs.

Mrs Connors commiserated. All pregnant women had periods of crying. I mustn't sit up there by myself. 'Come on downstairs! Bring your sewing. You don't? Well, I'll teach you!'

When does behaviour cease to be rational? One August day after Italian class, without any prior intention to do so, I walked into a boarding house with a 'Room for Rent' sign in the window and left ten dollars to hold the space till evening. It was the afternoon of Mrs Connors' weekly canasta game. It took me two hours to pack and carry books and suitcases downstairs. I left two notes. One to the Connors, thanking them for their many kindnesses and pleading the three flights of stairs as the reason for leaving. The other – much harder to write – to John, with the address of the boarding house.

It took the week's food money for a cab to transport our belongings to the new location. The single room – up four flights – looked out on a brick wall. It was hot, threadbare, and shared a bathroom with two other rooms.

But it had a door.

If I was baffled by my own precipitous behaviour, John was more so. Despite the patriarchal language of our marriage contract, we'd always before made decisions together. And here I'd moved us, bag and baggage, without even a discussion.

'We'd paid through September!' he kept saying when he arrived, bewildered and angry, after another day's fruitless pavement pounding. 'Why couldn't you have stuck it out just a few more weeks?'

How could I explain it to John, when I didn't begin to understand it myself?

Stopgap

'I have an interview with an insurance company tomorrow,' John told me when he reached our fourth-floor room one evening. Selling insurance wasn't what he wanted to do, but after knocking on publishers' doors for four months and the baby due in five weeks . . .

John took three days of tests and was offered the job over some two dozen other applicants.

'It's only a stopgap,' he told my parents the following weekend when we took the train out to Scarsdale. The four of us were at the dinner table. 'Just for a few months, till we start sending pieces from Europe again.'

'Stopgap?' My father set down his fork. 'A long time ago I took a stopgap job . . .'

He'd been twenty years old, Daddy went on, living with his family in New York City, where his father was preaching against Wall Street. As usual the pews emptied swiftly, and it fell to Daddy and his brother Raymond, the two oldest boys, to see their younger brothers and sisters through school.

'Like you,' Daddy said, 'I was going to be a writer . . .' A piece of his past I'd never known. 'I'd even sold a couple of stories.'

Then on the opposite side of the country occurred a cataclysmic event. Just before dawn on April 18, 1906, the city of San Francisco was rocked by a massive earthquake. Eighteen hundred people died, thousands of buildings collapsed. With gas and water mains ruptured, fire broke out, raging unchecked for three days and destroying many more buildings.

Insurance companies in New York, facing ruin in the wake of the disaster, recruited a small army of investigators. Their task: to sift through four square miles of fire-charred rubble, determining in each case whether a structure had been shaken apart by the quake and only afterward burned – an 'act of God' for which the insurer was not liable – or whether it had withstood the shocks and collapsed as a result of the fire, for which the company would have to pay.

Daddy and Raymond joined scores of young men boarding trains for San Francisco with a list of downed buildings to locate. 'That job was a stopgap measure, too,' he said. 'Just till my writing earned more.'

Much to their own surprise, the two brothers turned out to have a knack for deduction, spotting clues others had overlooked. Their reputation preceded them back to New York, where they began to be called in on police cases.

'Raymond enjoyed the work. I didn't.' But it was regular money coming in. 'The 'stopgap' has lasted forty-five years. My writing's packed away in a box in the attic.'

He turned to his son-in-law. 'Don't give up the dream, John.' If John was worried about me and the baby starving, 'I can use you as a shadow anytime you say – tomorrow morning if you like.

'Somewhere out there,' Daddy said, turning back to his cold dinner plate, 'there's a writing job with your name on it.'

New Look

What that job with John's 'name on it' would prove to be, none of us – Daddy least of all – could have guessed. It's only looking back that most of us can read the signposts to heaven.

John turned down the insurance job and continued standing in those lines of out-of-work writers. Days when the help-wanted columns listed no editorial openings at all, he worked for the Schindler Bureau as a shadow. Only an experienced operative, of course, can trail a subject on foot. John's work consisted of sitting in a car in sight of a warehouse door or occupying a rented room across from a restaurant under surveillance. One whole day he sat in a hotel room recording the precise moment when the phone rang in the room next door. The work was mindless and monotonous, dispelling any notion John may have had about the glamour of detective work.

In September Mother's parents arrived from Florida for their annual six weeks' stay in Scarsdale, timed for the end of the baseball season, when Papa never missed a Yankees home game. Goggie – the best my infant tongue had been able to do with 'Grandmother' – had been knitting a layette for her first great-grandchild, tiny sweaters, caps, and booties in noncommittal yellow.

Now Goggie made a despairing inventory of *my* wardrobe, stored in Scarsdale until I could get into my clothes again. While we'd been in France, the New Look had arrived in the States: voluminous jackets, skirts stretching six inches below the knee – a reaction to the fabric shortages of the war years. I'd never bothered about styles, but Goggie got out the sewing machine and set to work.

The New Look . . . if it had been only clothes, Goggie's needle would have set things right. But there was about to be a new look to every aspect of our lives. A new setting and new roles – for me that of a housewife in 1950s suburbia. And thus I stepped into the dragons' lair itself.

The Note

What a difference it would have made if I'd known that 'the place where the dragons lie' is on the road to the joys of heaven! In 1950, though, I was still travelling unaware . . .

I came upon Mother's note recently, saved with other cards and notes that came following the baby's birth. Affectionate and cheerful, it is not, after all, the shattering document my memory had made it. Two things, I think, made my reaction to it so out of proportion.

One was my immaturity. This was long before I could see my mother as a rounded person, with her own childhood history, her own strengths and needs. The other was the hours of unassisted labour the previous day – hours that neither she nor John, not even Dr MacKenzie, knew anything about.

All summer I'd been reading about the then-new concept of 'natural childbirth'. Apparently the staff at the hospital in Manhattan had not. 'If you want to do it without medication,' said the nurse on the maternity floor when I arrived at 2:00 a.m. on October 2, 'then we can't help you.' She took me to a small room, gave me a gown, got me onto a high hospital bed, raised the metal sidebars, and left, shutting the door with a decisive click behind her.

And on that bed I thrashed as the hours passed and the pain worsened. Whether they couldn't hear my screams or thought that such agony was what these peculiar natural childbirth enthusiasts expected, I never knew. The pain was multiplied by terror. Alone in that steel-barred bed, I became convinced that it was impossible for a baby to squeeze through a two-inch gap in solid bone. The baby and I would die together!

Downstairs in the waiting room, John had been told that it would be twenty-four hours before the baby came. In the dismissive way fathers were treated then, he'd been told to go home. 'We'll call you in time to get back before she delivers.'

Three days earlier he and I had moved from the boarding house to a better apartment at the same rent in Fleetwood, a twenty-five-mile train ride from the city. Perhaps the hospital really didn't think the baby would come that day, but when the phone rang in Fleetwood at 3:00 that afternoon, it was Dr MacKenzie, who'd arrived himself barely in time, to tell John that a healthy little boy had arrived.

'Your wife's fine too,' Dr MacKenzie said.

And so I was, in that miracle every mother knows, transported in a single instant from pain to joy; I held little John Scott and would gladly have done it all ten times over.

But the hours of lonely terror, as I say, doubtless exaggerated my reaction to what happened the following day. I had chosen this particular hospital for its 'Rooming In' option. Utterly inexperienced, I wanted to solve the mysteries of nappies and baths before heading home. With the baby in my room, only the same two visitors could be admitted during the five-day stay then standard after childbirth. It would be John, of course, in the evening hour, and for the afternoon one I'd asked Mother to come.

I'd put a fresh gown on Scotty the next day for the first afternoon visiting hour, when a nurse's aide came in with the note.

> *Darling,*
> *This is such a busy week that I've nobly*
> *given up my visiting privileges to John's*
> *mother. I know how fond you are of her,*
> *and isn't she the lucky one to see baby*
> *Scott before I do! We're all so thrilled at*

> *the news!*
> *Much love,*
> *Mother*

I understood – my mind did, anyway. Mother and Daddy had just moved from the house in Scarsdale where they'd lived so long to an apartment in the city and were still settling in. She *was* busy. But somewhere inside, another, older voice was crying, *Where is my mother?!*

In any case, I burst into tears, and at that moment Mother Sherrill stepped through the door.

John's parents had also recently moved to New York City, where Dad Sherrill had taken the Chair of Religious Education at Union Theological Seminary. Mother Sherrill stopped in the doorway.

'You were expecting your mother,' she said.

And because there was no use pretending, I simply nodded, and the tears passed as I enjoyed her delight in her first grandchild.

But . . . sitting in the armchair holding Scotty after she left, I reflected. Mother Sherrill was also a very busy person. She too was moving into a new home and just that week had started teaching a class at Barnard College. Yet each afternoon on the stroke of the 2:00 visiting hour, she appeared in the doorway with fresh flowers or a book or a box of scented soap.

Where is Mother? Some deep anxiety, some ancient wound, had been pried open, and spells of depression, sudden, overwhelming, were part of the new look of my world.

The White Picket Fence

Soon after Scotty's birth, John did take a stopgap job. At least this one was in the writing field, and it was only for a while, till we could get back to doing travel pieces. In December, with the baby two months old and every mail delivery bringing reminders of unpaid medical bills, John had answered an ad placed by a new little inspirational leaflet called *Guideposts.*

'A *religious* leaflet?' I'd asked dubiously when he told me he'd applied.

'I know,' he said. 'Not something I'd want to do for long, even if I get the job.'

Applicants were asked to supply samples of their writing, and in

January the editor, a man named Len LeSourd, phoned to say that John was their first choice. John had made it clear on his application that he was not a believer. 'You know what Len said?' John told me as he hung up the phone. 'He said, "That doesn't worry me a bit. If there's anything to the faith this magazine proclaims, belief will come in its own time."'

And so we settled into the routine shared by millions of other young American couples in the 1950s. Every morning John caught an early train into the city while I did the breakfast dishes and hung a row of nappies to dry on the shower-curtain rod. We had a cot, a baby carriage, and a stack of bills. Every cent left over from John's pay cheque, we'd agreed, would go into a savings account for those return fares to Europe. But months and then years passed, and there was never anything left over.

Four decades later, in 1990, I attended a planning session for *Virtue,* a Christian women's magazine, at a mountain retreat in Oregon. The other editors were bright young professional women and mothers; one of them nursed her infant during the discussions. I listened for two days as they spoke of the pressures of juggling family and career, condemned our selfish, materialistic culture, and looked back wistfully at the wholesome world of the 1950s. I remember the startled circle of faces when I broke in at last with an emotional description of what the fifties were really like.

I was startled myself at the force of my feelings! Today's materialism, I heard myself say, is nothing compared to that of the fifties, because then it was unquestioned. In a decade when millions of displaced people in Europe lacked basic shelter, the American woman was praised for attending exclusively to her own little house in its segregated neighbourhood behind its white picket fence.

The function of the 1950s housewife, I told them, was to *buy.* It was a new consumer culture of toaster covers and laundry *whiter! brighter!* than your neighbour's. One popular ad showed women discussing in shocked whispers a wife whose husband's shirts on the backyard clothes-line revealed 'tattletale grey'. We were to keep a sharp eye on each other for all such evidence of imperfect housekeeping and nonconformity.

Because that young editor was nursing her baby during my outburst in Oregon, I used this issue as an illustration. Breast-feeding, when my children were born, was condemned as a holdover from an unsanitary past. Bottles and formulas were the modern way. 'And don't forget,' my paediatrician would caution, 'to weigh him on the infant scales before and after each feeding'. Infant scales sold for $39.95 – the equivalent of hundreds today.

'I tried anyway to nurse all three children,' I told the Oregon gathering. 'And I failed three times.' If the baby was fretful, or if I had so much as a sniffle, the doctor would warn that my primitive insistence on breast-feeding was endangering my child's welfare. I was ignorant of everything about mothering, only holding onto some half-formulated notion of 'naturalness'. And the natural was to have no place in the dawning plastic age, when products were to meet all needs.

Today I understand better the reasons for all this. America had just fought a global war at immense cost in lives and resources. With husbands and sons home from foreign battlefields, every instinct drew us to our own needs. And the huge industrial capacity of the United States, built up to wage the war, had to find an outlet in consumer goods.

Massive output requires a mass market, standard products for standard customers. Today too I know that in the fifties there were many, many women like me, isolated in our look-alike houses, each guiltily believing herself the only one failing to feel the fulfilment the media assured us was ours.

'Listening to you discuss the problems facing women today,' I told the group in Oregon, 'I kept thinking, *Praise God, they're talking about these things!*' In the 1950s women were not allowed to have problems that could not be solved with the right purchase.

My unhappiness in the fifties, of course, had personal causes as well. The landscape of our individual journey is always a mix of public features and private ones. In my case, the contrast between the wide world of travel writing and the confinement of housekeeping was too sudden, even if I hadn't been lugging baggage from childhood.

Eventually Dr Kazan, the psychiatrist I'd begun seeing in 1951, helped me to see that the role of housewife held special menace for me. My mother too, I began to understand, had needed a barrier between herself and other people. Mine was that mythical door, hers was housework. Whenever, as a child, I'd tried to talk to her, she'd remember ironing she hadn't done or a room that needed vacuuming.

Since Mother had household help, I think I knew even then that housework was her way of hiding. I of all people should have empathised! Instead I blamed the cooking and the mending and the silver polishing for her unavailability. *I* would never give importance to such things.

In fact, I kept writing all through the fifties. But at a price! Scotty was five months old when I found an editing job I could do at home. Every few weeks the Updegraff Press would mail a book manuscript for me to work on. The mail slots in the apartment lobby, however, were letter-sized; the bulky manuscript envelopes would lie on the floor in sight of inquisitive neighbours. Soon it was rumoured that the inhabitant of 15A was 'different' – a fatal word in those days – and the friendly greetings in the hallway ceased.

The harm of 1950s stereotypes, though, was mostly self-inflicted. It wasn't so much that others condemned me, as that I condemned myself. Except for those few months before and after Scott was born, I have always worked – and until our youngest entered high school in 1971, I did it under a cloud of self-reproach. Combining career and family was a juggling act indeed, as the women in Oregon said, but for those of us who attempted it in the 1950s, it was a problem each one wrestled with alone.

The Attic Room

John's temporary job at *Guideposts,* meanwhile, was proving more intriguing than he expected – meeting interesting people, learning about their lives, even if he didn't buy into their religious concepts. The small editorial staff was overworked, and by Scott's first birthday I was doing interviews for the magazine on weekends, writing them up at night.

In 1954, when our second son, Donn, was nine months old, we moved to a circle of identical small homes in Mt Kisco, a New York suburb another twenty miles farther north. It was there in the autumn of 1955, pregnant with our third child, that I reached the crisis point. Part of it may have been hormonal, part was certainly grief over my father's death the year before, part an ever-growing sense of inadequacy.

Already seeing myself a failure as a housewife, I began to believe I was failing as a mother too. As much as I hated ironing and mending and cleaning, I loved everything directly to do with our two little boys. Feeding, watching, teaching, learning from Donn and Scott, brought me the most intense joy I'd ever experienced.

But more and more often out of its cavern crept the old dragon of self-rejection. *Me?* Responsible for the nurture of these eager, shining, beautiful beings? As my depression deepened, it seemed to me that anyone and everyone else – the passerby on the street – had more to give our children than I did.

At last the dragon chased me upstairs to a small room in the partly finished attic, where there was a daybed and an actual door. And there I lay while a succession of baby-sitters managed, I was convinced, so much better than I could. In fact, to me, my death seemed the way to remove my potentially harmful presence. The memory he can't shake, John says, is of coming home from New York each night to find me in that attic bed, face turned to the wall.

More than a bed, I think now that the attic couch was a cot into which I tried to crawl, an unconscious reversion to that ten-month-old infant. Tragically, in crying out for a missing mother, I took a mother away from my own children. At the time, it was simply inconceivable to me that I had value for anyone. How often ever since, though, I've looked back and grieved for the hurt to two little boys! Scott was in nursery by then, but for two-year-old Donnie, the centre of his world was on the other side of that closed door.

The Shopping Trolley

By the time Liz was born in February 1956, Dr Kazan had found medication that allowed me to function, and the worst of the crisis was over.

It was a shaky equilibrium at first, and the place of greatest threat was the supermarket. Simply stepping inside, I'd feel the panic rise. So many choices! Shelf after shelf, aisle after aisle . . . In the indecisiveness that marks depression, I could find no reason to prefer one item over another. I would pause and consider, walk on and return, grab something, put it back, select something else.

When the pounding of my heart grew too strong, I'd lift Liz from the shopping trolley, seize Donn by the hand, and flee to the closed-in safety of the car. Beside me on the seat, Donn, two-and-a-half, would regard me solemnly:

'We forgot the food again, Mommy.'

Dr Kazan made a commonsense suggestion that at least kept us from starving: 'Find a small grocery store.' I located an out-of-the-way place where a taciturn clerk retrieved orders with pincers on a pole from tall shelves behind a counter.

'Got no vegetable soup.'

'Well . . .' (oh, the relief from deciding!) 'just give me what you have.'

I developed a repertoire of such devices to get me through routine tasks. Unable to confront the blank page at the start of a new story, I took to writing between the typed lines of previous work. I ran errands when stores would be emptiest, pretended a toothache because I could not smile. I was getting through the days, but it was hardly living.

The Entrance

Holy Cross is a Benedictine monastery on the Hudson River thirty-five miles north of our home, where I go from time to time for a day of reflection on my journey. Looking back to those days when I travelled in darkness, I wonder why my unhappiness itself didn't show me my need for God. Here both John and I were, writing for a publication whose whole thrust was to show that God had answers to far more serious problems than mine.

But it was not my problems, apparent though they were, that led me to the kingdom. And the monastery building itself reminds me that our journeys seldom unfold so predictably. The three-storey brick structure sits on a hillside, its gracious entrance facing the Hudson. From this entryway the architect designed a broad driveway leading down to an imposing riverside dock.

But the driveway and dock were never built.

In 1902 when Holy Cross was erected, it was taken for granted that people would arrive by steamboat. Carriage roads were dusty or muddy according to the season, and passenger trains didn't serve the west side of the river. Steamboats – fast, modern, dependable – were the obvious choice.

As for the faddy, funny-looking 'auto-mobiles', they were too new, too few, too experimental for the planners at Holy Cross to take into account.

Those daily steamboat runs between New York and Albany must have seemed as changeless as the tides that sweep up the river from the sea. The monastery's builders never questioned positioning the entrance to face the water. Before the pilings for the dock could even be sunk in the riverbed, however, automobile highway construction had begun. And for a century, people have been entering Holy Cross through the back door. It's a small service entrance, originally designed for local farmers arriving with their horse-drawn produce. But this is the humble door monks and seekers have always used to enter the hallowed space. How do we enter heaven? The answer is almost always a surprise.

By 1956 I was a full-time *Guideposts* employee, working from home. For five years I'd interviewed people about their personal faith. Heard about illness healed, financial needs met, relationships restored. Surely this would be the door through which both John and I would step into another dimension of experience.

In fact, almost the opposite was true. It was not that I disbelieved what people told me. Just that it never occurred to me to apply it to myself. One interview was with an Olympic skier, another with a coal miner . . . a stunt pilot . . . a movie star . . . a rodeo clown. I didn't have these people's talents, so why should my spiritual life be like theirs? Answered prayer, miraculous guidance – these were exciting things that happened to others. I might have a pang of longing: *Wouldn't it be great to believe like that!* No different from other fleeting wishes. *Gee, wish I could ski like that!*

Actually, when it came to religion, John and I prized our outsiders' status. Interviewing all persuasions of Christians from Roman Catholics to Free-Will Baptists, we could identify with each in turn. 'Objectivity' we called it. 'Fence sitting,' said our Christian friends.

Our very ignorance, we insisted, made our writing clearer. Statements that might go unquestioned by a fellow Christian – 'God told me to make that phone call' – drew a barrage of *hows* from John or me. How did God tell you? How did you know it was God?

If we were content with our agnosticism, however, others were not. In the course of some interviews we'd be preached at and prayed over, coaxed and condemned, until in self-defence we learned to adopt the religious passwords of the group we were with.

Some passwords, that is. Others grated so I couldn't bring myself to utter them. One formula in particular irked me, till I was willing to lose a story altogether rather than reply when someone accosted me with,

Have you been saved?

This black-and-white division of the human race into 'ins' and 'outs' contradicted everything I'd observed since coming to *Guideposts.* No two histories I'd heard were alike, no two encounters with God the same. 'How can they talk as if "saved" were a switch – on or off!' I'd splutter to John.

Another question religious people posed, though, I could not dismiss: *What about your children?* Weren't we going to give Scott and Donn and Liz any exposure to religion? To biblical literature? Why not at least send them to Sunday school so that, later, they could make an informed decision?

That argument struck a chord in my Unitarian conscience. And so in the spring of 1956, John and I began to look for a local church.

The Search

'The church affiliation of the husband will constitute the church membership of his dependants', I quoted our marriage certificate. Since John had been raised in the Presbyterian church, we started there. Then Methodist, Congregational, Baptist, Church of Christ, and so on, some thirteen churches in four towns, a couple of Sundays at each.

At first we tried going as a family, but with children aged five, two, and three months, I spent most of the service retrieving crayons from under the pew. So John started going one week, I the next, then comparing notes.

'Really friendly people.'

'They certainly made me feel welcome.'

'They couldn't have been nicer.'

Sunday after Sunday, outstretched hands, smiling faces, and . . . 'Where shall we try next?' What we were looking for we didn't know, just that we weren't finding it.

What we did find was a new verb, *fellowship.* 'So glad you could fellowship with us today.' We were invited to fellowship at coffee hours and discussion groups, potluck suppers and Thursday night couples' clubs. We were pressed to attend men's breakfasts and women's luncheons.

The end of the experiment came for me six months after it began. I was leaving a steepled, white-clapboard, Norman-Rockwell-painting of a church, trying to recall the points in the sermon to repeat to John, when a woman in a red felt hat seized my arm. 'The church fair is next month will you make an apron?' she asked. All one sentence.

She must have thought I was either deaf or dim-witted as I blinked at her without a word. The truth was, I was fighting tears. It was not yet a year, at this point, since the days when I'd been afraid even to step past the door of the little room upstairs, and my confidence was still fragile.

Will you make an apron? evoked my losing battle to acquire the skills 'every' woman of the 1950s possessed. Sewing especially . . . when I tried to poke a piece of thread through the miniscule hole in a needle, it frayed into a hydra-headed monster.

I don't remember how I answered the lady in the red hat. I do know I almost ran to the parking lot, away from the smiling people, away from the outstretched hand of fellowship. John kept up the church search for another month, but the impetus had gone out of it for both of us. Our Sundays reverted to yard work and the *New York Times*.

I believe, in fact, that writing for a religious publication made our spiritual journeys harder. Working with Christian subject matter acted as a kind of inoculation: exposure to a safe dose of the germ to prevent our coming down with the real thing.

Exposed we were, constantly. We knew secondhand about reaching the bottom of the pit and finding God there. About miraculous supply. About the inner voice that guides. We'd lived all these things vicariously as we helped people put their stories on paper.

And on paper, for us, they remained. The challenging sermons we'd heard during our six months of church hunting had lost the force of impact. We had been immunised.

Silence

The road to heaven, for both John and me, was a different one.

On the northbound side of the New York State Thruway in the Bronx is a gas station that I never pass without recalling a snowy January night in 1957. The station is closed now, its fieldstone walls disfigured with graffiti, but I still see it as it looked on the winter night we pulled in to use the telephone.

John and I and other *Guideposts* staffers had attended a Salvation Army fund-raiser where the speaker was the presiding bishop of the Episcopal Church, Henry Knox Sherrill. After his talk we joined the long line waiting to shake his hand. John mentioned the coincidence of the name, and he and the bishop briefly compared family histories.

It was after 10:00 p.m. when we walked to the parking garage and got in our car. While we were at dinner it had begun to snow.

'Could be bad up our way,' said Norm Mullendore, *Guideposts'* art director, as he climbed into the backseat. Norm lived near us, forty miles north of the city.

It was bad even before we got out of Manhattan, snow mixing with sleet, traffic crawling. By the time we reached the Bronx, we knew we wouldn't make it home before midnight as we'd promised the sitter. 'We've got to call Mrs Coolidge,' I said.

Norm thought there was a gas station not far ahead. 'If it's open.' At last through the sleet pelting the windshield we saw the welcome lights of the station. 'Tell Mrs Coolidge just to open the sofa and go to bed,' I called as John got out of the car.

He was inside the station a long time.

'Maybe the phone lines are down,' Norm said.

At last we saw John coming toward the car. Instead of getting in, however, he simply stood there in the storm. Norm rolled down the back window. 'Couldn't get through?'

'I got through. Mrs Coolidge had a phone call from my mother. Dad died at 9:30 this evening.'

For a while there was only the sound of ice crystals pinging against the roof of the car.

But . . . we'd been with Dad two days ago! Sixty-four years old, excited about the upcoming semester at Union, he and Mother had taken the train out to our house Sunday afternoon. As always, I'd served my one confident casserole: kidney beans, sliced potatoes, crumbled bacon, tomato soup. I could hear Dad's warm, deep voice, 'I always look forward to this.'

Dad couldn't be dead!

John had gone back to the station to call his mother. Back in the car he reported their conversation. 'They went out to dinner,' he said. 'The restaurant wasn't far and you can never find a taxi when it snows, so they walked back to the seminary. They read for a while, Dad in his leather chair with the Braille Bible in his lap. Then Mother went to the kitchen to make cocoa. When she came back with it, she thought he'd fallen asleep . . .'

Mrs Coolidge had volunteered, John said, to stay overnight. We drove Norm to Fordham Station to catch a northbound train, then turned the car around and headed back to Manhattan. *What can we possibly say to Mother?* I agonised as we followed the snowploughs back into the city, too stunned to speak much even to each other.

Why, this coming weekend Dad was going to baptise Liz! The ritual meant nothing to John and me, but since Dad kept asking about it, we'd settled on her first birthday for the service.

It was 1:00 a.m. when we found a parking place on 116th Street and took the elevator up to the apartment in McGiffert Hall. Two students at the seminary had moved Dad from the library onto his bed – he was a light sleeper and he and Mother had separate bedrooms. The undertaker would arrive at 8:00 in the morning.

John and I had come, but as I feared could find nothing of comfort to say. The Sherrills had never been huggers or touchers; they expressed love with words. On that terrible night words would not come for any of us.

'You've got to get some sleep, Mother,' John said at last. 'There'll be a lot to do tomorrow.'

Mother came to the door of the guest bedroom with a nightgown for me. For a long while I lay awake, wondering why such verbal people as the three of us should find that words deserted us when they were needed most.

I was wakened in the predawn dark by a shriek. I ran into the hall to find Mother sobbing in the kitchen doorway. I put my arms around her – the first time I'd ever done so. Her alarm had gone off at 6:00 as always, she said when she was able to speak, and she'd gotten up to start the coffee.

'I was tiptoeing,' she told me. 'He sleeps so lightly, you know. I was trying not to wake him.'

It was just before 7:00 when the door buzzer sounded. I opened it to see Reinhold Niebuhr standing in the hallway. I sighed with relief. A fellow professor at Union, this renowned theologian would have the consoling words John and I had failed to find.

'Come in! I'll go and get Mother.'

Translator of the ancient German 'serenity prayer', Dr Niebuhr was known for his gift of phrasing: God grant me the serenity to accept those things I cannot change, the courage to change those things I can change, and the wisdom to know the difference. *What eloquent words this man will find at a moment like this!* I thought as I returned with Mother and John.

With the four of us seated in the living room, I waited eagerly for Dr Niebuhr to begin speaking. A minute ticked away on the antique clock. Two minutes, while my expectation mounted. At last, with knobby arthritic fingers, Dr Niebuhr reached for Mother's hand.

'Well, Helen,' he said – the very first words he had uttered.

Silence fell again. Five minutes . . . ten full minutes went by, and still this gifted speaker had not shared his words of wisdom.

The clock chimed a quarter past seven. Something remarkable was taking place among the four of us. As the stillness of the room seeped inside me, a wordless communion seemed to enfold us all. When the clock sounded the half hour, Dr Niebuhr stood up and let himself out.

And still John, Mother, and I sat silent. A staggering question was taking shape in my mind. Dr Niebuhr's silence – was it . . . about God? Had he brought with him something about faith that could not be said? Something about presence? About being?

Our being here last night.

A nightgown.

A hug.

These weren't religion, these were . . . just things people did. Was God those things too, things beyond language? For six years now, at *Guideposts,* I'd pressed people to talk about God. I'd put their words – thousands and thousands of them – on paper. Could God be found outside of words?

Not until the undertakers arrived at 8:00 did any of us speak, and then only to deal with the logistics of death. Later, other words would come. Words of honouring and love that John and I needed to speak in their time. Letters would come from across the country and the world, even a note from Bishop Sherrill saying that he'd read the news in the *Times* and recalled tracing family roots the night Dad died.

The question remained with me, though. A question about silence, chosen over words by one of the great wordsmiths of our century. Two years later, silence would be the door through which I would step into the courts of heaven.

Heaven around Me

No heaven can come to us unless our hearts find rest in it today. Take heaven.

Fra Giovanni, 1513

O world invisible, we view thee,
O world intangible, we touch thee,
O world unknowable, we know thee,
Inapprehensible, we clutch thee!

Does the fish soar to find the ocean,
The eagle plunge to find the air –
That we ask of the stars in motion
If they have rumour of thee there?

Not where the wheeling systems darken,
And our benumb'd conceiving soars!
The drift of pinions, would we hearken,
Beats at our own clay-shuttered doors.

The angels keep their ancient places:
Turn but a stone, and start a wing!
'Tis ye, 'tis your estranged faces,
That miss the many-splendoured thing.

But (when so sad thou canst not sadder)
Cry – and upon thy so sore loss
Shall shine the traffic of Jacob's ladder
Pitched betwixt heaven and Charing Cross.

Yea, in the night, my Soul, my daughter,
Cry, clinging Heaven by the hem;
And lo, Christ walking on the water,
Not of Gennesareth, but Thames.

Francis Thompson, In No Strange Land

The Hand Holder

Thou dost hold my right hand.

Psalm 73:23 RSV

On the wall of my mother-in-law's bedroom in Louisville, Kentucky, hung a framed quotation in hand-lettered Gothic script:

I said to the man who stood at the gate of the year;
'Give me a light that I may tread safely into the unknown.'
And he replied, 'Go out into the darkness and put your
hand into the hand of God. That shall be to you better than
light and safer than a known way.'

More than fifty years ago, when I went to Louisville to meet my new in-laws, I would step into that room, read these lines by Minnie Louise Haskins, and puzzle over them.

The words in that frame seemed to me the embodiment of everything Unitarians rejected. An anthropomorphic deity (how could anyone hold the 'hand' of God!). Blind faith (why should being led around in the dark be better than stepping out in the clear light of reason?). Such outmoded religious notions, Aunt Helen had assured me, were believed only by ignorant people.

My mother-in-law, Helen Sherrill, however, was not ignorant. An author and authority on early childhood development, she must have thought this enigmatic quote important to hang it where her eyes would light on it first thing each morning.

Later, when Mother and Dad Sherrill moved to New York City, the Haskins quotation hung on the wall of her bedroom there. It hangs today in my bedroom. In the years since I first read those words, I've become an adherent of that 'outmoded' religion. And I've come to see in Haskins' prose-poem the traveller's guide to heaven.

Our hand in his is of course a poet's way of expressing trust. And why should dark be better for our journey than daylight? Because, I've come to feel, holding our hand is God's delight.

Oh, there are practical reasons, too, why he cannot banish the darkness here and now. Light – his Light – would show us too much. In 1991, an operation was performed on a blind man named Virgil. For forty-five years, neurologist Oliver Sacks reported, Virgil had functioned effectively as a sightless person. Suddenly able to see, he was overwhelmed by a torrent of impressions bombarding a brain that could not process them. He became disoriented, listless, miserable. When an illness destroyed his new-won vision, Virgil welcomed the return of blindness.

'Now, at last,' wrote Dr Sacks, 'Virgil is allowed to not see.'

Allowed to not see . . . If we were suddenly able to see as God sees – the entire past, the entire future, the ultimate consequence of each thing we do, each word we speak – perhaps we too would be unable to cope. Perhaps in his compassion God *must* keep us in the dark.

But I think his hand-holding goes far beyond mere necessity. In the 1960s when our kids were teenagers, a Beatles song throbbed through our house: 'I Want to Hold Your H-a-a-a-nd', came through the closed door where I'd be trying to work, till I'd end up holding my ears.

But I believe God sings the same refrain. I think he longs to keep us company, to walk at our side like a lover, hand in hand. I think he doesn't reveal the future to us, not only because we couldn't handle it, but because if he did we'd drop his hand and race ahead alone. 'Thanks! I see how to get there now!'

Getting there, even to some noble goal, is not as important to God, I suspect, as the journey in companionship with him. It's relationship, not achievement, that he wants.

This is the opinion, at least, of one of the greatest achievers I know. Andrew van der Bijl, 'Brother Andrew' to millions, is a Dutchman, today in his seventies, who for over forty years has been bringing the good news of God to places where Christians 'cannot' go, first behind the Iron and Bamboo Curtains, today in the Muslim world.

When John and I were writing *God's Smuggler,* the story of Andrew's adventures, we began by asking about his accomplishments. How many Communist countries had he worked in? How many people had he reached? There were impressive answers to all this, but Andrew thought they were the wrong questions. These weren't the things he wanted people to remember. 'What I hope someone will say about me some day is what the Book of Genesis says about Enoch, "Enoch walked with God."'

It's an hour by hour, minute by minute thing, Andrew said. 'God doesn't set us a task and come back later to see how we've done. He goes with us every inch of the way.' And it's along the way that the important thing happens, the creature falling in step with the Creator.

Enoch walked with God. Andrew spoke it like an invocation, like a four-word prayer. 'If that could be said of me, it's all the reputation I'd ever want.'

The Ten-Week Experiment

I'm sorry that it took me more than thirty years to meet this God who walks at our side. In the Unitarian church I'd learned about God's majesty, his moral demands, his truth reflected in many traditions – and I'm forever grateful for these insights. But . . . to imagine this infinite God giving individual attention to just one of billions of human creatures on a speck of a planet at the edge of a minor galaxy?

Because I couldn't imagine it doesn't mean of course that he wasn't attending to me, every moment of my life. An infant has no concept of the mother who holds him. But I stayed an infant so long! How much joy I missed by failing to perceive his arms beneath me. How much I still miss when I fail to see him throughout the day.

Heaven lies around each of us, closer than the air we breathe, this very moment. It's the growing awareness of this immanent heaven – like all human awareness, always partial, always capable of more – that I've come to see as the single Christian story, whatever the difference in details.

The details are important too, though. It's in the specifics of our stories that we discover just how personal God's dealing with us is – so tailored to each alone that there are as many ways of taking his outstretched hand as there are individuals.

For me, the awareness began with that cross-country car trip in 1959.

That June, as soon as school was out, we'd piled the kids, ages eight, five, and three, into our grey Ford station wagon and set out to zigzag twelve thousand miles across the country, interviewing interesting people.

President Truman in Missouri. John Paul Stapp in New Mexico, 'the fastest man on earth,' who rode a rocket sled to simulate bailing out of the new jet fighters. Alfred Hitchcock in Los Angeles. Governor Mark Hatfield in Oregon. Homesteaders in Alaska.

In between these scheduled stops, we did what we'd done ever since our first writing trips in Europe, typewriter strapped to John's bicycle. Go to a local newspaper office and ask to see the 'morgue', the storeroom where back issues of a paper were kept in the days before microfilm.

We'd emerge with ink-blackened fingers and the account of a tornado . . . a factory fire . . . a missing child. In Virginia we went to see a man who'd been lost in Dismal Swamp. In Alaska, a teenage boy blinded by a bear. Though the news stories didn't mention faith, we'd found, in interviewing for *Guideposts,* that every survivor has spiritual discoveries to share.

The homeward leg of the trip was different. No interviews, no combing newspaper files, just long hours in the car as we pushed to get back for the start of school. To the drone of the tyres, all three children would often stretch out on the mattress in the back and fall asleep. And John and I found ourselves with that rarity in the lives of young parents, time to talk.

We discussed upcoming book projects. How to stretch our budget to include guitar lessons for Scott. What would happen when President Eisenhower met face-to-face with Khrushchev. Montana . . . North Dakota . . . Minnesota . . . Could Liz wear Donn's outgrown snowsuit this winter? Would my brother's job with General Electric in Havana be affected by this new name in the news, Fidel Castro?

We were in Pennsylvania, almost home, and the topic of religion – religion as it affected us personally – had not come up. By this time we'd been writing for a religious magazine for eight years without ever making that personal connection. But since we'd covered the important subjects, we got around even to this one. We hadn't been inside a church, I realised, since the apron episode more than two years earlier.

'What do you believe now,' I asked John, 'about – well, God and everything?'

'I haven't really thought about it. What about you?'

I hadn't thought about it either. 'If only there were a church somewhere,' I mused aloud, 'where people would leave you alone. Let you have your own experience, if you're going to have one.'

An unfriendly church, John agreed, was what we needed. Five miles passed in silence. 'How about Episcopalians?' John said.

'Aren't they supposed to be "God's Frozen People"?'

But were there any in our area? There was a handsome stone church in Mt Kisco, just past the statue of the Indian chief who gave the town its name, that we thought might be Episcopalian. We hadn't ventured into it during our months of church hunting – the parking lot seemed to be full of Bentleys.

Signs for resorts in the Poconos. We'd be home by nightfall. 'Why don't we try it for a couple of weeks?' I suggested.

'Maybe,' said John, 'two weeks isn't long enough.'

And on the last few miles of the long trip, we established two rules for the new experiment. We'd go to the church by the Indian, starting that coming Sunday, for ten weeks. That would be . . . we counted up. Till Thanksgiving.

And, the all-important second rule: We wouldn't talk about it.

Like all verbal people, we could wring an experience dry with words. Just as we hoped no one in the stone church would talk to us, we agreed not to discuss our reactions with each other either, until Thanksgiving.

The Golden Cross

> 'Lo, I am with you always'
> means when you look for God,
> God is in the look of your eyes,
> in the thought of looking.
>
> *Rumi, thirteenth century*

We almost forgot that conversation in the pressure of unpacking and assembling enough clean clothes to get Donn off to first grade, Scott to fourth. But on Sunday, an overcast, drizzly September morning, we drove past the statue of Chief Kisco and pulled into the parking lot of what turned out, indeed, to be St Mark's Episcopal Church.

There were just the two of us, the children after the long separation from friends being inextricable from various neighbourhood homes. We followed a stream of dauntingly well-dressed people through a small stone anteroom and a wood-panelled vestibule, into a dimly lit sanctuary.

I was looking down at my travel-weary blue skirt and wishing I'd worn my best shoes even if they hurt, when I glanced up and stopped short.

I was staring at a bit of medieval England. From where I stood, the centre aisle led past thick stone pillars to a magnificent carved-wood screen. The aisle continued through the screen, up three stone steps, past some choir stalls, and up still more steps to a stone altar. In Aunt Helen's Unitarian church, the central aisle ended at an imposing pulpit. But in this Gothic gem, the aisle led to that altar. And in the centre of the altar was a golden cross.

John was gesturing to me and I realised I was blocking the doorway. We slid into the last pew, safely near the exit. A lady in a stylish black straw hat sat down next to me, pulled a maroon velvet cushion from beneath the pew in front of us, and dropped to her knees. With some apprehension I saw that every single person, on arriving, did the same, kneeling for a moment with bowed head.

And still my eyes kept tracing that route down the middle of the room, through the carved screen, past the choir stalls . . . On that rainy autumn morning the rest of the church was a shadowy place of grey stone, the brightest spot, the focal point, that gleaming cross.

What are you going to do about me? it seemed to ask. *Either what happened on the cross is central, or it makes no difference at all.*

The question didn't come to me that crisply that day. I only knew that the architecture of this church was speaking to me as words never had.

Now from a side door came a teenage boy in a white cassock, carrying another cross atop a tall wooden pole. Behind him filed a black-and-white-robed choir. The congregation stood, and I noticed that as the cross passed each pew, the people bowed.

Last in the procession came the minister, taking a seat just beyond the wooden screen. A tall, elegant figure framed by that Gothic carving, he appeared to me to have been designed right along with the church. Only later in the service did we learn that this was his first Sunday at St Mark's too.

For the next quarter of an hour I was busy juggling hymnal, service leaflet, and a black-bound *Book of Common Prayer,* which for the lady in the black straw hat seemed to open mystically at the proper place for the different responses. There were times when people stood, which we imitated, and times when they knelt, which we did not. At last the minister – 'rector', the leaflet called him – mounted a handsome carved-oak pulpit to the right of the carved screen, and we settled back for a respite from a very athletic style of worship.

'Before I begin,' the Reverend Marcus Hall said, smiling down at the congregation, 'I would like to dispel a rumour. I've heard it said that St Mark's has a reputation as an unfriendly place.'

John and I exchanged hopeful glances.

'From those parishioners I've already had the privilege of meeting,' the rector continued, 'I'm sure there's no truth to such an allegation. I would like everyone here to turn right now and shake hands with the person next to him.'

From where John and I sat in the last pew, we could see the entire sanctuary. And in that whole congregation, nobody moved. Not a head turned. On all those ladies' hats, not a feather quivered.

The Reverend Hall waited for an endless painful moment, then snapped on the pulpit light and picked up his sermon notes. What was going through his mind as he faced that stone-still room, I don't know. Nor what was in the minds of those who'd declined his invitation. I only know that in the back of the church, two people rejoiced at having come to the right address.

The Mesh

> Heaven, now there's a thought. Nothing has ever been able, ultimately, to convince me we live anywhere else. And that heaven, more a verb than a noun, more a condition than a place, is all about leading with the heart in whatever broken or ragged state it's in, stumbling forward in faith until, from time to time, we miraculously find our way . . .
> – It is laughter, I think, that bubbles up at last and says, 'Ho, I think we are there.' And that 'there' is always here.
>
> *Alice Walker*

Looking back on that rainy September Sunday today, more than forty years later, I can only think that God in his mercy worked a very small, very personal miracle on behalf of that pair in the last pew. I believe today in that kind of condescension from the God of the universe. And this belief has been formed and nurtured over the years at that same St Mark's Church.

That we should have gone there that Sunday, of all days. That Marc Hall, who became a lifelong friend, should have made that particular appeal, and that two hundred people should have been deaf to it, as though God had placed his hands over their ears. These things show me his pursuit of each individual person as though only that one mattered.

John and I, fugitives from fellowshipping Christians, running scared of people with designs on our souls, made the acquaintance of this God Sunday after Sunday in that stone-pillared space where God permitted no one to invite us to a church supper, no one to ask me to sew, no one to speak to us at all.

As agreed, we didn't speak about these Sunday mornings to each other either. For me it was a week by week discovery of the mesh between me and a particular church tradition. From stories I'd worked on, I knew that such meshes existed. The inner-city kid reached by a tough-talking street preacher. The businessman responding to the workplace language of Norman Vincent Peale.

But that God should have a way to connect with me too – that was the wonder of St Mark's. First of all, there was a book to hold. As I learned to find my way around in the *Book of Common Prayer,* I began to grasp what a treasure chest of many centuries' devotion it is. But it wouldn't have mattered, to start with, what was between its covers. Any book, for me, was security.

And the language of this particular book! Much of the English in that 1928 edition dated back to Shakespeare's day – and I'd been a Shakespeare major.

Though it was a long time before I could kneel without self-consciousness, other acted-out elements of the service spoke to something totally unsuspected in me. The cross carried in procession, the candles, the priestly robes, the genuflecting – the ceremony of it all!

In the lucid and rational services of the Unitarian Church, with their appeal to the best in humankind, something, for me, had been missing. The numinous. The irrational. The acknowledgment of the worst in us. It was as though, within a life centred on the effort to understand, there was another self. Passionate, illogical – the kind of person I thought I didn't like.

I remember an evening service at St Mark's eighteen years after we stepped so tentatively through its doors, when someone put into words what I'd sensed, that first day. I'd been wanting my music-loving friend Sandra Aldrich to hear St Mark's glorious organ, but her own Baptist church met at the same Sunday morning hour. This unusual evening Eucharist, a memorial service for our late assistant rector, Father Brinckerhoff, was my chance to invite her.

Two minutes into the service I knew it was a mistake. Father Brinckerhoff, it seemed, had been an Anglo-Catholic, perpetually frustrated by St Mark's low-church style. To honour him that evening, St Mark's had decided on an unprecedented High-Church mass. There was chanting in Latin, swinging of censers, ringing of bells, sprinkling with holy water.

Through clouds of incense I stole increasingly anxious glances at my Baptist friend, sitting very erect through all the kneeling and bowing. It was unlike any service at St Mark's before or since, though I doubted I could explain this to Sandra.

'Well,' I ventured, when choir and clergy had processed a final time about the church and the acolytes had snuffed out the last candle, 'I don't know what all of that said to you.'

'What it said?' Sandra echoed. She turned to me eyes bright with tears. 'It said, "the *holiness* of God".'

Holiness.

That was what I'd felt, that rainy September Sunday in 1959, though I'd lacked the word for it.

Long before that service for Father Brinckerhoff, John and I had discovered in 'unfriendly' St Mark's the loving community that's been our extended family ever since. We'd met there people of every economic level. A few rich – the ones whose cars in the parking lot had caught our eyes. A few poor. Most in between. For us St Mark's came to be not a church building but a place where the church – the people of God – gathers to worship.

Did St Mark's change? Or did we? Did God simply shield us, until we were ready for it, from the warmth that was always there?

Whatever the explanation, in 1959 we were not ready. As we adhered to our programme of attending the grey stone church till Thanksgiving, we needed to be left alone and we were. For ten weeks, in a small act of God's grace on our behalf, we attended the 11:00 service each Sunday without anyone approaching us.

We stuck to our own no-talking-about-it rule too. The power of silence, the God-beyond-words I had glimpsed through Reinhold Niebuhr, was doing its mysterious work. Thanksgiving came and went and, still without discussing it, we continued going. We never did have that end-of-experiment talk. We simply found ourselves, Sunday mornings, getting Liz into a dress, the boys into jackets and ties, and heading for St Mark's.

We were a very long way from personal commitment or an encounter with Christ or any such thing. Those were to come for each of us in different ways. But since that September day in 1959, except when travelling, we have not missed a single Sunday at the stone church beyond the Indian.

The Road to Compostela

The worshipping life is a journey that leads to the experience of paradise. We discover by God's grace that we have always been in our Father's house and heart.

The Rev Ralph Peterson, interim pastor, St Mark's, 1995–96

It was at St Mark's that I began to think of my life as a pilgrimage. I'd encountered this concept years earlier – and rejected it.

It was in 1955, as my depression deepened, that John's parents had come out from the city for dinner. With the heightened perception of the blind, Dad Sherrill was unusually sensitive to people's moods. His question to me that day, however, seemed dismally unrelated to mine.

'Have you ever heard,' he asked, 'about the treadmill, the saga, and the pilgrimage?'

When I said I had not, he explained that these were the three basic ways of looking at our lives. The *treadmill* sees existence as meaningless, an endless round of activity repeated over and over. I looked at the sink full of dishes, the laundry piled on the washing machine. I could relate to treadmills!

The *saga,* he went on, while agreeing that life is basically without purpose, sees nobility in the way people cope. Heroes of all cultures, from Homer's *Ulysses* to John Henry who died with a hammer in his hand, live out the drama of human courage. *Nothing heroic,* I thought, *in my defeat before ordinary domestic challenges.*

Only in the *pilgrimage,* Dad concluded, is life, all of it, past and present, the good, the bad, the seemingly indifferent, seen as going somewhere. The pilgrim is not simply reacting to events around him or her – a child with mumps, the next payment due on the car – but seeing beyond and through these things to a goal. The particulars of daily life become stepping stones to a destination.

In 1955 the concept of pilgrimage was even more alien to me than the heroics of a saga. How could I concern myself with some way-in-the-future goal? My problem was how to get through the next twenty-four hours.

The conversation stuck in my mind, however, and as the clouds began to lift, I started to read about pilgrims, especially accounts from the Middle Ages, when pilgrimage meant a literal journey. There were three principal destinations, I discovered, for the millions who took to the roads – Rome, Jerusalem, and Santiago de Compostela.

Like many seekers, John and I, in time, went to Rome and Jerusalem. But these trips, in medieval times, would not have made us pilgrims. People who'd been to Rome were 'romeros', those who went to Jerusalem, 'palmers', from the palm branches they brought back. Only travellers to the remote shrine of St James at Compostela in the northwest corner of Spain were 'pilgrims'.

The more I read about this most demanding of the three journeys, from Paris nine hundred miles across mountains and forests, the more it seemed to me the perfect pattern for the pilgrimage of the spirit. And so in 1999 as our millennium ended, John and I set out to retrace – in the comfort of a car – the route taken by pilgrims in 999 at the close of the last millennium.

In a trip filled with discoveries, the most surprising one, for me, came at the very beginning. The staging area for pilgrims setting off from Paris, we'd learned, was the church of St-James-at-the-Butcher-Stall. All that's left of it today is the bell tower, the *Tour St Jacques*, the Tower of St James, with a small park around it. Why, this was the very spot where we'd so often come with lunch makings when we lived in Paris in the late 1940s!

From the little park in 1999, John and I walked the pilgrim route across the Seine and through the Latin Quarter on the *rue St Jacques* – once just a street name to us. Old maps indicated a hospice nearby for travellers bound for Compostela. Only the sanctuary connected to the hospital remains today – another Church of St James. Coming to it, John and I exchanged looks of astonishment: The church was half a block from that walk-up apartment where I'd felt the waves of nausea as I climbed the stairs.

We'd walked past this church every day, taken the first steps along the old pilgrim way countless times. And had never seen the road to Compostela literally beneath our feet. And I thought of Dad Sherrill's words, so meaningless to me once, so significant now. Whether my life is treadmill, saga, or pilgrimage depends not on where my feet are, but where my heart is.

The Hymn

> **Author of the World's joy,**
> **Bearer of the World's pain,**
> **At the heart of all our distress**
> **Let unconquerable gladness dwell.**

> *Dag Hammarskjold*

Life as a pilgrimage, heaven its goal . . . Unlike those medieval journeys through space, however, the moment we put our foot on the road to heaven, we're already there!

For nearly two thousand years one hymn has opened the act at the heart of Christian worship. The Lord's Supper, Eucharist, Holy Communion, Mass, by whatever name the sacrament is known, it begins with the Sanctus. *Sanctus, Sanctus, Sanctus* chanted in Latin, *Holy, Holy, Holy* said or sung in a thousand modern tongues, not just here on earth but as the old prayer book puts it, 'with Angels and Archangels, and with all the company of heaven'.

> **Holy, Holy, Holy, Lord God of Hosts,**
> **Heaven and earth are full of thy glory!**

For decades now I've repeated these words with other Christians at least twice a week, often every day. Thousands and thousands of times as I prepare to take the Lord's Body and Blood, 'Holy, Holy, Holy . . .'

For a long time, though, one word of the Sanctus was impossible for me to say.

Full.

'Heaven' to me was still a theoretical realm. A place 'full of thy glory' sounded suitably vague and lofty. But earth? Earth was real —

containing much that was glorious, but also much ugliness and tragedy. How could earth be 'full' of God's glory?

Yet the church insists on it. 'Our bounden duty', in the old prayer book's wording, is to proclaim the Sanctus 'at *all* times, and in *all* places.'

For years I wrestled, as Christians have through the centuries, to reconcile my dawning belief in God with the all too obvious existence of evil. I'd weigh my fledgling faith against the calamities in the daily paper – murders, floods, earthquakes, war. My faith always lost these intellectual battles.

Meanwhile, though, through the individual men and women who shared their stories with me, I was encountering a different reality. Good experienced in the very clutches of evil itself.

Clyda Holbrook and her husband were stabbed by the thieves who robbed their motel. Though permanently disabled, Clyda survived; her beloved husband did not. But the woman I met in Eureka, California, far from being bitter, was launching a 'love-wave' in her community to counter the crime-wave that had taken her husband.

Chet Bitterman's twenty-eight-year-old son, a missionary in Colombia, was kidnapped and murdered by terrorists. The young man left a wife, two small children, unfulfilled dreams. But when I visited his father in Lancaster, Pennsylvania, I didn't hear about vengeance. I heard that his son's memorial fund was going to provide the ambulance needed by a Colombian village.

Edith Taylor's husband of twenty-four years obtained a mail-order divorce in order to marry a nineteen-year-old. But the day I called on Edith in Waltham, Massachusetts, her home rang with the laughter of two little girls and glowed with the love between two women. The other woman was the husband's second wife. When his death left her and their two small children destitute, Edith took all three into her heart and home.

Listening to a hundred stories like these, I kept seeing that cross shining at the end of the aisle at St Mark's. The cross, tool of death, symbol of life everlasting. The cross where the vertical of heaven intersects the horizontal of a suffering world.

The Closet

For Father Samuel Brinckerhoff, to whose memorial service Sandra Aldrich had come, this heavenly intersection was everywhere.

We were very new Christians; he was a very old one. Ordained in 1907, Father Brinckerhoff had come to St Mark's in his retirement, assisting there till his death at nearly ninety. White-haired and stooped, he seemed to me to move about the church in a little personal patch of sunlight. An office had been created for him in what had been a storage closet – barely room for a small desk and chair.

I don't remember what took John and me to this tiny office to see him one day, I only recall that to receive visitors, he had to stand and push the chair to the desk. Whatever our errand, the conversation soon turned, as every conversation with this happy man did, to the joy of the Lord.

Maybe angels felt this joy, I remember thinking, *but where is the evidence of it in the real world just now?* This was during our national agony in Vietnam, when the word *overkill* had entered the language. After walking for years in unavailing peace marches, I'd become disillusioned about humankind's ability to stop killing one another.

'There may be joy in heaven,' I said to the old priest, 'but where do you see it here on earth?'

Father Brinckerhoff turned his mild blue eyes on mine. 'On earth?' he repeated. 'But – ' he flung his arms as far apart as they would go in the narrow room, '*this* is the kingdom of heaven!'

Looking at him as he stood in his little pool of radiance, I knew not only that I'd met someone who believed unshakably in a real heaven, but that he was already inhabiting it.

Ever since, my favourite image of heaven has been a cramped little room and a man with the light of eternity in his eyes.

The Waiting Room

> Our eyes do not see you, but we have this excuse:
> Eyes see surface, not reality.
>
> *Rumi*

'*This* is the kingdom of heaven!' Father Brinckerhoff's words launched me on a lifelong experiment: trying to discern heaven right where I am.

Sometimes it's easy. Driving through the Rocky Mountains when the aspens are turning yellow. Stepping into St Thomas Church on Fifth Avenue, the wall behind the altar thronged with saints ascending. In such places heaven seems to shimmer just behind the visible world. In others . . .

One of the tough places for me is Memorial Hospital in New York City, where John and I go for his annual cancer checkup. The world's premier cancer centre, Memorial is a bewildering complex of buildings on Manhattan's upper east side. The Head and Neck department is on the third floor of Sloane-Kettering. And there, in a waiting room facing a row of examining cubicles, John and I have now spent some three hundred hours.

'Waiting' room is right; never less than two hours, often as many as four, while nurses and doctors, adept at avoiding eye contact, emerge briefly from one cubicle and disappear into the next.

What makes this place an especially unlikely precinct of heaven is that in this unit everyone's medical problem is visible. There are bandaged eyes, swollen cheeks, lopsided jaws – in John's case a scarred neck and a partially missing ear. There we sit, patients and family members, isolated in our separate fears. Tables hold magazines, but few people pick them up. Some talk in lowered voices, some hold hands. Most simply stare, unseeing, at reproductions of Van Gogh apple trees on the walls.

I pretend to look at the pictures too as I study the people in the room. Today on our right are two bearded Hassidim with long sideburns and flat black hats. Father and son, I decide. To our left sit an elderly black couple. Beyond them two women in saris whisper over the bandaged head of a little boy. Old and young, we gather in this room from all over the world. In that way, at least, Memorial Hospital is like heaven. No nation or race excluded.

Patient records today are computerised, but in a drawer of the appointment desk is one old-fashioned file card, ragged with years of handling. 'We wouldn't throw John's card away for anything,' the receptionist tells me. John is one of the survivors, in his late seventies now, in his mid-thirties when we first sat in these chairs.

As I gaze surreptitiously about the room, I am praying for each of the patients waiting with us, that they too will live to become as familiar with this third-floor room as we are.

'What can you tell me about that person?' my detective father used to test my skills of observation. 'Look at hands first, then posture, then clothes.' As I pray I try to picture homes, families, occupations. My mental images are guesswork, of course, but one thing I can spot for sure: those arriving for the first time. They clutch an instruction sheet from the admitting office downstairs, often pinned to a sheaf of records from other institutions. Their eyes widen at the sight of the surgical scars on their fellow patients, then look swiftly away. Watching these newcomers, my mind goes back to our own first time here, when we knew nothing about cancer, still less about prayer, only a chill, mind-numbing fear . . .

It was in January 1957, almost three years before that first Sunday at St Mark's, that I'd noticed a small mole on John's left ear. When I pointed out that it was growing, he shrugged. Trying to get John to a doctor was like trying to get the children to eat liver – wasted breath. At last, going for an insurance checkup, he promised to get it looked at.

'What did the doctor say?' I asked that evening.

'It's nothing. He said he'd remove it for cosmetic reasons if it bothered me.'

Cosmetic. If there's a word that can make a stubborn man dig his heels in harder, I don't know it. Week after week I watched the angry-looking growth darken. Week after week my 'pestering' got nowhere. With kids ages six, three, and one, he pointed out, we had enough medical bills without running to a doctor out of vanity. Psychiatry bills, too, kindness kept him from adding: I was seeing Dr Kazan at this point three times a week.

Finally in September, because I kept bugging him, John had the thing off in a brief office visit at our local medical centre. 'Satisfied?' he said when he came home with a Band-Aid pasted to his ear.

It was a good day all around. Dr Kazan had just that morning agreed that I could stop taking the medication I'd been on for nearly two years.

Two days later I answered the telephone. It was the doctor who'd removed the mole. He'd like to see my husband. Yes, right now. And, uh – perhaps I could come with him? Well, bring the baby along.

At his office a mile from our home, the doctor shoved a lab report across his desk. As a matter of routine, he explained, he'd sent the tissue for a biopsy. It was malignant melanoma, a particularly fast-spreading cancer of the lymph system. If it couldn't be checked, John might have as little as three months. He'd made an appointment for John that afternoon with a specialist at Memorial Hospital.

Practical steps. Phone the baby-sitter. Collect the tissue sample from the lab. Pick up Donn at nursery school. Leave a note at Mt Kisco Elementary: 'Mrs. Coolidge will come for Scott today.'

By 3:00 John and I were threading our way for the first time through Memorial's maze of hallways – so like the unmarked road looming ahead in our lives. Don't look down it! Take a step at a time. Find the right department, fill out the forms.

John was seen by the chief of Head and Neck, Dr Daniel Catlin. Three days later, Dr Catlin removed a slice of John's left ear and the lymph tissue on the left side of his neck.

John remained in the hospital for a week. Both our fathers were gone by then, and I didn't yet know my heavenly Father. So I reached out to my grandfather, up from Florida for his annual end-of-the-baseball-season visit. The day after the surgery I poured out to him my fears, the uncertain prognosis.

'I'm seeing a doctor next week too,' Papa said. 'I have an acid stomach. My doctor in Miami gave me a prescription, but I don't believe it's helping.'

On and on, the recital of Papa's ills, Papa's medications. My beloved grandfather – at age eighty his world had narrowed to the horizons of his own needs. It was a growing-up passage for me, just then when so much growing up was asked. To see Papa not as I needed him to be, but as the central figure in his own story, with a childhood, a young adulthood, failures and successes. In time it meant a deeper, more adult love for him, but that night it was another of life's props knocked away.

Looking back, I see the tremendous good that flowed for both John and me from this terrible time. See, for example, how our props, one by one, *must* be left behind on the Way that is Jesus. To put our faith in anyone or anything else is to let go of his hand.

'What seemed when they entered it, to be the vale of misery,' C. S. Lewis writes about the souls in heaven, 'turns out, when they look back, to have been a well. And where present experience saw only salt deserts, memory truthfully records that the pools were full of water.'

But that 'present experience', that salt desert time, when one has no suspicion that there *is* a heaven! The simplest daily act was clouded in fear. Tucking the children in at night – would they grow up without a father? Stepping into the supermarket, not so long before a place of terror – what if the panic attacks returned? None of this could I share with John, of course. My job was to be upbeat and encouraging and run the water in the sink to mask the sound of crying.

Even out of this, good would come: a lifelong empathy with the partner in a crisis – the competent, smiling, supportive one with the hollow place inside. That very month I happened to be writing about a munitions worker who'd lost his hands in an explosion. I remembered how during the interview I'd thanked his wife for the coffee, turned to her for details of his rehabilitation, and not once asked what the upheaval in their lives had meant to *her*.

The Question

It is God to whom and with whom we travel, and while he is the End of our journey, he is also at every stopping place.

Elisabeth Elliot

To know that good will come – this is to perceive heaven around us here and now. I have a friend who learned to do this in a salty land indeed. For fifteen years Barbara Holmes suffered excruciating back pain that nothing relieved, not medication or acupuncture or biofeedback or eight surgical operations. In her pain Barbara learned to listen to God and to write down his promises.

In 1996 she had a miraculous healing. Long before this, though, good had come to Barbara in that ability to hear God. She continues to write down the messages she receives 'because I know they're not just for me.'

She didn't know I was writing about journeys when from her home in Delaware she sent me the message she'd heard on March 10, 2000.

The path you see is crooked and bent and crowded with weeds. And you feel detoured and confused. But the path you see as crooked, I see as straight. In spite of the obstacles, I see you on the path headed straight to me. Do not despair about the crookedness. For in the bends I place great blessings.

John and I did not know about the 'blessings in the bends' as he began those monthly checkup visits to the third floor of Sloane-Kettering. It became a kind of ritual. Always both of us together: Line up Mrs Coolidge, take a fistful of coins for the parking meter. No silent prayers, in those days, for the others waiting with us. Just: *That woman . . . the whole side of her face . . . what if . . .*

Go with John at last into one of the cubicles with its wall charts of head and neck anatomy. Watch, scarcely breathing, while Dr Catlin adjusts the light on his metal headband and grips John's tongue between squares of gauze. Practised fingers probing the neck. 'Okay. See you in a month.' And to celebrate, calamari at a restaurant on Second Avenue.

In March 1959, two and a half years after the surgery, the time between checkups was extended to six months. That was the summer of the long car trip and the decision to attend the grey stone church near the Indian.

When the date for the second six-month checkup rolled around the following March, we broke our routine for the first time. It was Parents' Day for Scott's fourth grade. His story about a ferocious wolf was up on the wall, he informed us, with *six* stars on it.

'You've got to be there,' John told me. 'Silly for both of us to spend all afternoon sitting around a waiting room anyway.'

I drove him to the train station – there'd be no one to keep running out to feed the meter. 'Call me when you know what train you'll be coming out on,' I said.

He phoned around 5:00. 'I'm catching the five-twenty,' he said in what he probably supposed was a casual tone. 'Gets to Mt Kisco at six-sixteen.'

John is the world's worst actor. Before he got three words out, I knew that the news, this time, was bad. He was to enter the hospital next day for a second operation.

Again, the boon of things to do. Go to the phone, cancel dates. One call was to *Guideposts'* editor, Len LeSourd, to tell him we wouldn't make the editorial meeting that week. Early the next morning Len's wife, Catherine Marshall, telephoned. Could we come over for a few minutes? – the LeSourds lived around the corner.

Both John and Catherine have written about the conversation that morning in the LeSourds' family room. Driving over, John and

I expected the usual commiserations, a promise to pray, perhaps an offer of help with our kids, the same ages as their three.

Instead, Catherine put to John the question that all his life, growing up in a clergyman's home, writing stories of other people's faith, attending St Mark's Sunday after Sunday for the previous six months, he had avoided confronting.

'John,' she said, 'do you believe that Jesus Christ is God?'

It was an immensely important question, she went on. Perhaps the only question that mattered. 'An eternity in heaven hinges on your answer.'

I kept my eyes fixed on the dark TV set across the room, the screen as black as my fears. I didn't want to think about heaven! Heaven was what people talked about when someone was dying.

'I'd feel like a coward,' John answered Catherine. 'To come running to Christ with my tail between my legs when I'm scared.'

'John,' Catherine said urgently, 'that's pride. That's wanting to come to God in your own time, your own way. Maybe this is Jesus' time, Jesus' way.'

It wasn't writing Christian articles that made someone a Christian, she continued, or going to church, or living a moral life. It was answering that question. John brought up a lot of arguments, and Catherine was buying none of them. At last I reminded him of the time. We'd asked for an appointment at 9:00 with the rector of St Mark's.

John thanked Catherine for her concern, and we hurried out to the car. We'd gone about half a mile toward the church along winding Millwood Road when John broke the silence.

'Well, I've done it.'

'Done what?'

'What do they call it? Making a "leap of faith"? I believe that Jesus is God.'

For another half mile neither of us spoke. 'What does it feel like?' I asked at last.

John thought for a moment. 'I guess it feels a little like dying.'

The Side Chapel

> Come, my Way, my Truth, my Life!
> Such a Way as gives us breath,
> Such a Truth as ends all strife,
> Such a Life that killeth death.
>
> *George Herbert*

Marc Hall was waiting for us in the wood-panelled rector's study at St Mark's. Urbane, scholarly, he spoke eloquently about the role of faith in the crisis confronting us.

'I was wondering,' John broke into the flow of words, 'if you could say a prayer for me. I mean, for God to heal me.'

The Reverend Hall looked – just for a moment – taken aback. 'Why, of course,' he agreed. He picked up a *Book of Common Prayer* from his desk. 'There's a prayer right in here for such occasions.'

For a while the only sound in the room was the turning of pages. 'Here it is. "Unction of the Sick." Let's go into the sanctuary.'

In the shadowy church Edgar Hilliar, the organist, was rehearsing, sonorous chords echoing from the stone walls. The Reverend Hall stepped behind the communion rail in the small side chapel while John and I knelt on the long needlepoint cushion. In front of us, above the altar, a Tiffany window depicted St John's vision of the glorified Christ in heaven. The morning sun on the glass illuminated the words above Jesus' head. *I Am the Resurrection and the Life*.

Raising his voice above the organ, Marc Hall began to read. 'I lay my hand upon thee, beseeching the mercy of our Lord Jesus Christ . . .' A priest reading a prayer from a book, John who'd been a Christian perhaps fifteen minutes, and me, wondering if the bathrobe I'd washed for him to take to the hospital was dry yet. '. . . that all thy pain and sickness of body being put to flight . . .'

Marc's voice boomed out in a sudden silence from the organ. '. . . the blessings of health,' he concluded more softly, 'may be restored to thee.'

Suiting his action to the words, Marc shifted the prayer book to his left hand. 'I lay my hand upon thee,' he read again as he placed his right hand on John's head. Beside me I felt John's body give a jerk.

And unaccountably, I began to cry.

Edgar Hilliar was playing again. John stood up, Marc Hall stepped out from behind the railing. Wonderingly, I saw that both of them were fighting tears too. There was an awkward silence, some mumbled farewells, no one meeting another's eyes.

We drove home in silence. Later John told me that at the touch of Marc's hand a bolt of intense heat coursed like an electric shock down the side of his neck, stopping there, searing, burning, then travelling clear to the soles of his feet.

It was hours before he could speak about it. In silence we packed his suitcase for the hospital, each wrestling with the knowledge that something extraordinary had been present in that chapel. Something we couldn't name or describe, a reality that fit nothing we knew.

When Dr Catlin operated the following day, in John's neck where the newly discovered lump had been, he found instead a tiny heat-shrivelled residue. Not a tumour, but something more like a cinder.

The Light

> **Whether I fly with angels, fall with dust,**
> **Thy hands made both, and I am there;**
> **Thy power and Love, my love and trust**
> **Make one place everywhere.**

George Herbert

'*All* the way to heaven is heaven.' But to know this when things go wrong takes a faith we didn't have. This second surgery, the one that was to produce such good news medically, was for both John and me, living through it, a kind of hell.

I remember sitting in the busy visitors' lobby of Memorial Hospital's surgical wing, watching the clock on the wall circle through the slow minutes of the operation taking place somewhere on the floors above. Surgery was scheduled for noon and would take an hour and a half, maybe two hours, Dr Catlin had told me, depending on how much he had to remove. He would phone the desk here in the lobby when it was over to give me a report, probably around 2:00.

Two o'clock came. The seats in the lobby changed occupants. Three o'clock. How radical was the surgery turning out to be! At 3:30 I spoke again to the crisp and efficient lady at the desk. Yes, she had my name. Yes, she knew where I was sitting. I returned to my corner of the leatherette sofa, not daring to venture even as far as the coffee machine in the hallway for fear of missing the doctor's call.

Four o'clock. The crowd in the lobby had thinned. Dr Catlin must simply have forgotten to phone. John had to be in the Recovery Room by now! There was a new face at the desk. She was sorry, she did not have that information. At 4:30 from a phone booth in the hall, I called Dr Catlin's office. The doctor was not in. No, there was no message for Mrs Sherrill. I called the office again at 5:30 and got his answering service.

'The office is closed. You can call tomorrow morning at nine.'

My desperation must have sounded in my voice. Protesting that she was not authorised to do so, the answering service operator gave me Dr Catlin's home number. A woman answered. No, the doctor had not come home. No, she didn't know when to expect him.

It was five past six when I was summoned at last to the desk in the lobby. It was Dr Catlin, who'd left the operating room ten minutes earlier. The neck surgery had gone well. 'But we had a little trouble on the operating table.'

John had been sedated, he went on, and the anaesthetist was inserting the breathing tube into his throat, when both John's lungs collapsed. Dr Catlin had done an emergency tracheotomy. From the exhaustion in his voice, I understood that a life-and-death battle had been waged over John's unconscious form. While I was wondering why he did not call, Dr Catlin had been fighting for John's survival. Only at 4:30, about the time I began calling his office, when John's vital signs were normal again, had the actual surgery begun.

And John? He woke that night in the Intensive Care Unit to the worst pain he had ever experienced. From a hole in his throat and from both sides of his chest poked plastic tubes. Around him machines whirred and bubbled. No one thought to explain to him that the multiple incisions were not, as he of course assumed, because the cancer had spread throughout his chest.

Morning came; the pain worsened. And the second night, into the midst of the pain, strode Jesus.

He came as light, piercing the wall of the room. Light impossibly bright. Alive, conscious, infinitely knowing, infinitely loving. Two days earlier John had acknowledged, without understanding, that Jesus was God. Now, still without understanding, he saw him.

And John did what seemed inevitable in that luminous presence. He asked help not for himself but for others there in the ICU – an old man who could not stop coughing, a young man who moaned. The coughs and the cries stopped.

John's own pain did not go away. It simply ceased to matter in the wonder of an all-encompassing new relationship.

Later, John wrote about this experience. In response he's received some eighty letters over the years describing similar events. What strikes us most about them is that the Light, without exception, appears when the darkness is deepest.

'And the city has no need of sun or moon to shine upon it,' the Book of Revelation says of heaven, 'for the glory of God is its light' (Rev. 21:23 RSV).

John was in heaven that night, and he was in the surgical wing of a cancer hospital, and it was the same place.

The Cup

> **If I ascend up into heaven, thou art there:**
> **if I make my bed in hell, behold, thou art there.**
>
> *Psalm 139:8 KJV*

God present in pain as truly as in joy.

One of my favourite authors is Henri Nouwen, that wise and gentle Dutchman who lived with a community of the mentally disabled. When he planned to join John and me and several other writers on Cape Cod for a few days of sharing, I looked forward to meeting him at last.

Illness made him cancel those plans, an illness from which he did not recover. Because there were so many questions I'd wanted to ask him, I read with special eagerness his last book, published the month before he died.

In *Can You Drink the Cup?* Nouwen writes of 'the Cup of Sorrow'. Famine, epidemics, child prostitution, in his global travels Nouwen had grieved over all of them. He lived daily with the sorrows of the mentally handicapped. And he had his own times of depression and doubt.

'There was a time,' he wrote, 'when I said, "Next year I will finally have it together," or "When I grow more mature these moments of inner darkness will go."'

Christian maturity – this was the very subject I'd hoped to ask him about! I too was always waiting for unwanted traits to fall away. Someday I wouldn't have these cyclic depressions. Someday I'd be more outgoing. Someday I'd get my desk cleaned up.

'But now I know,' Nouwen continued, 'that my sorrows are mine and will not leave me.'

I read the words with dismay. Here was a modern-day saint who to the very end of his life could not eliminate the negatives in his personality. 'The adolescent struggle to find someone to love me . . . unfulfilled needs for affirmation . . . sorrow that I have not become who I wanted to be. They are very old and very deep sorrows and no amount of optimism will make them less.'

But there's a surprise about this Cup, Nouwen went on. 'The cup of sorrow, inconceivable as it seems, is also the cup of joy.' He could not explain the mystery; he could only experience it. 'In the midst of the sorrows is consolation, in the midst of the darkness is light, in the midst of the despair is hope.'

In the *midst* . . . simultaneously . . . in the very worst moment. I thought of John in the ICU. Thought of the darkest times in my own life, and saw myself at such moments turning to God, gaining compassion, growing.

And if I refuse the Cup? If I will not make peace with the flawed person I am – what then?

Maybe, I think, carrying on in my head the conversation I never had with Henri Nouwen, *it's not my flaws that stand between me and heaven. Maybe it's that ideal image of myself. That serene, loving, well-organised creature-that-never-was.* The effort to be perfect, Nouwen's insight suggests, may be hell's biggest temptation.

My friend Lucia Ballantine gave me a verse by Leonard Cohen that I've taped to the side of my still heaped-up desk:

> **Ring the bells that still can ring.**
> **Forget your perfect offering.**
> **There is a crack in everything.**
> **That is how the light gets in.**

The Ladder

The gate of heaven is everywhere.

Thomas Merton

It was a regular midweek service in the side chapel at St Mark's. I took a chair there, as I had perhaps a thousand times in the thirty-six years since Marc Hall laid his hand on John's head in that same chapel. Sunlight filtered through the Tiffany window onto the red-tile floor as a dozen or so of us waited for Father Ralph Peterson to enter.

The floor . . . row on row of brick-coloured tiles outlined in black. I'd never really looked at them, my eyes drawn instead to the white marble altar flanked with mosaic angels. Beneath my feet the regular squares advanced toward the altar rail. *Like a ladder,* I thought.

Why a ladder should have come to mind I don't know, but once it did, it was all I could see in the grid of the tile work. *I'm sitting at the foot of a ladder,* I thought, bemused. *A ladder leading to where the angels live in heaven.*

Father Ralph came in and the small congregation stood. He said the opening prayers, then looked around. 'I guess our scheduled reader's not here,' he said. He nodded at me.

'Tib, read the first lesson, will you?'

I stepped forward and took the Bible he held out. 'Genesis twenty-eight, verses ten to seventeen,' he said, pointing out the place on the page.

Jacob came to a certain place, I read aloud, . . . *and lay down in that place to sleep. And he dreamed that there was a ladder set up on the earth and the top of it reached to heaven . . .*

I stared at the page. Seconds passed before I looked up to see puzzled faces regarding me. Hastily I read on . . . *and behold, the angels of God were ascending and descending on it. . . .*

I forced myself to finish. *Then Jacob awoke from his sleep and said, 'Surely the Lord is in this place; and I did not know it. . . . This is the gate of heaven'* (Gen. 28:10–17 NRSV).

'You okay?' my friend Susan whispered as I sat back down.

I nodded, but my head was spinning. To see a ladder to heaven in a floor pattern and the next moment read about one . . . One friend calls such coincidences 'God-incidences' and believes they're intended to call our attention to something. At home I reread Genesis 28.

This is the gate of heaven. . . .

I had recently reread John Bunyan's *Pilgrim's Progress,* that epic allegory of humankind's quest for heaven. But in Jacob's story it's heaven that does the questing. *Could heaven be seeking us?* I wondered. *Longing for us to open our eyes and see the ladder thronged with angels rising right at our feet?*

Once more I read the Genesis story. Jacob at this point in his life is certainly no heaven-bent pilgrim. Quite the opposite – he's a fugitive from justice, running from the brother he has swindled. Preoccupied by his own fears, even after the vision of the ladder he makes no faith commitment. *If* God provides him with food and clothing, Jacob bargains, *if* God smoothes over the family feud, *then* Jacob will believe in him.

How like John's and my first visit in 1959 to the chapel with the red-tile floor. Frightened by the return of the cancer, running scared, not sure of what – if anything – we believed, we'd asked for prayer and stumbled onto the gate of heaven.

The healing of the cancer was a gate only, of course. Not the courts of heaven, far less the throne room. An entryway, a glimpse into a realm whose existence we hadn't suspected any more than fear-filled Jacob did when he lay down on the rocky ground with a stone for a pillow.

The Decision

> **Seek not to understand that thou mayest believe,**
> **But believe that thou mayest understand.**
>
> *Augustine*

For us, as for Jacob, fuller experience followed, an ever-growing awareness of God's presence. Much of this growth – for me especially – *has* involved effort. Always happiest as a student, having sighted this wondrous realm, I seized on it as a subject for study. A rationale for attending lectures and filling scores of notebooks.

In the years since Marc Hall and John and I stepped into that chapel, I've sat at the feet of great Bible teachers, read hundreds of Christian books, gone on long retreats, followed a daily prayer discipline, visited the great pilgrimage sites of the faith. Mine was not a leap of faith like John's, but more of a crawl.

For me the chief point of resistance was the Apostles' Creed, that recital of ancient dogma in the face of logic, science, and common sense. Listening to the preposterous words at St Mark's week after week, I could hear the voices of my family rising in protest. Mother's voice, perplexed. Aunt Helen's, indignant. My brother's and sister's, 'You're not serious!'

To assent to the Creed, to recite it myself, would be to turn away from a heritage I treasured. I would alienate old friends, too, I knew, if I became an actual believer in these strange claims. Confessing the Creed would not mean, to me, lack of respect for other beliefs. But in choosing for myself a Christian worldview, I would open an unbridgeable gulf between me and many I cared most about.

Like Mea Ivimey . . . Of all Mea's disappointments in me – my conventional suburban life, Little League, and the PTA in place of poetic isolation – nothing had distressed her so much as my growing interest in Christianity. When I'd first started attending St Mark's, she'd put it down to our active household. 'With the demands of the children,' she'd say, 'I can see why you'd enjoy a quiet hour.'

But to begin to *believe* the same thing all the others did! Her chief objection to Christianity seemed to be its popularity. How could her soul mate share a set of beliefs with millions of ordinary people? Each time I raised the subject, it was met with such a despairing shake of the head that I eventually stopped trying.

Despite objections without and qualms within, however, three years after the experience in the chapel, I made the forty-five-mile trip to New York's Cathedral of St John the Divine for the formal sacrament of confirmation. In the echoing vastness of the world's largest Gothic church, I spoke the Creed aloud for the first time. *I believe in God . . . and in Jesus Christ . . . born of the Virgin Mary . . . crucified, dead, and buried . . . rose from the dead . . . ascended into heaven . . .* For me it had been a faltering journey over my own prejudice, fears, and intellectual pride.

As I repeated the ancient formula, I understood John's comment on making his own decision that morning in the car three years earlier. It felt like dying.

New Birth

And with that 'death' came the birth of something new. In the years since that trip to the cathedral, a blessing pronounced each week by the minister has held special meaning for me.

Almighty God . . . by the power of the Holy Spirit keep you in eternal life.

The prayer is not that God will *give* us eternal life. It's that he will *keep* us in a life already begun, already being lived here on earth. And this life begins with the death of some little piece of self-will.

In these love stories, no two of which are alike, the holdout against the divine Suitor takes many forms. For me, reciting the Creed, for John, confessing that Jesus is God, for someone else, kneeling or praying aloud or something else. But when this clamouring, protesting little egotist is allowed to die, there's room where it was for the birth of something new.

The Light that John saw in the hospital has never returned, he says, in visible form. But the relationship begun there has persisted. John told me several years later that, while he was happy to be granted more years of earthly life, he'd been aware ever since that night in the ICU of another life unfolding alongside this one. One independent of daily ups and downs. When his mind doubted and his spirit sagged, the new life pursued its unshakable course.

I knew what he meant. I too catch glimpses of this parallel existence. The life that isn't dependent on me at all, the life I'm already living in heaven.

The Stoplight

> Heaven is not built of country seats,
> But little queer suburban streets.

Christopher Morley

The glimpses come when I least expect them. When I'm not studying, not praying, not trying to develop the discernment of a Father Brinckerhoff – not thinking about heaven at all. Just, all at once, there I am . . .

I was driving from our house to the village of Mt Kisco one

107

afternoon, as I do a dozen times a week, with the usual list of errands – a package to be weighed at the post office, dry cleaning to drop off. I was stopped by the traffic light at the edge of town. I was sitting at the wheel, watching the cars turn onto Route 133 from Maple Avenue, waiting for the light to turn and wondering how long the line at the post office would be, when suddenly . . . I was filled with a nearly unbearable love for the people in every car I saw.

It actually ached, the yearning for each of them was so strong. How gracious that driver signalling his turn! How patient the woman in the car behind him! How infinitely valuable every driver, every passenger . . .

The light changed and the moment passed. How long did it last – thirty seconds? It was as if for the blinking of an eye the curtain that shielded me from reality had lifted, and I'd felt a fraction of what God felt as he brooded over that intersection.

If the curtain had not dropped again at once, I think the intensity of feeling would have torn me apart. Nor could I sustain that love for other drivers; soon the roads filled again with tailgaters behind me and dawdlers in front. But for one indelible moment, an utterly ordinary scene had been, in a sense, unmasked: At the junction of Route 133 and Maple Avenue was the gate of heaven.

The Burning Bush

> **Earth's crammed with heaven**
> **And every common bush afire with God.**
> **And only he who sees takes off his shoes.**
>
> *Elizabeth Barrett Browning*

If the portals of heaven can swing open on a suburban street, they can open anywhere. It's new eyes, not new settings, that make the difference.

Take off your shoes! God cautions Moses as he approaches the burning bush. *The place where you are standing is holy ground.*

And where is this sanctified spot? Not in some splendid palace of Moses' youth. Not in one of the awesome Egyptian temples he knew so well. The holy ground is an ordinary patch of desert where Moses, as he does every day, is herding sheep. Just another rugged stretch of the wilderness where he's fled, like Jacob, to escape trouble back home. But because Moses stops and looks, he detects the presence of God.

What if our new-opened eyes saw in *every* bush the radiant world that permeates our own! What if, as Elizabeth Barrett Browning wrote, it's only our inattention that misses it?

And he looked, and lo, the bush was burning, yet it was not consumed. And Moses said, 'I will turn aside and see this great sight' (Exod. 3:2–3 RSV). It's the turning aside that makes the difference. Moses stops, he looks, he interrupts his daily activities. And only then does God reveal the sacredness of these seemingly commonplace surroundings. *When the Lord saw that he turned aside to see, God called to him out of the bush . . . 'put off your shoes'* (Exod. 3:4–5 RSV).

What if I could learn to see this whole earth as holy ground? What if wherever I looked I saw a ladder at my feet?

I've known people who do. Father Brinckerhoff was one. My friend Molly Shelley was another. Most of her life, Molly admitted, she hadn't been good at seeing even in the ordinary way. 'Would you believe,' she told me, 'that I never used to see trees? Really *see* them?'

Till the age of forty-two, Molly had been caught in that same perfection trap that lures me too into focusing on my performance instead of God's. She was busy trying to be the perfect wife, the perfect mother to her six children, the perfect Christian, always at church or Bible study, taking on every volunteer job in the parish. Then in 1981 Molly was diagnosed with inoperable cancer. Activities curtailed, she became aware of a voice that, she suspected, had been calling to her for years. *Come out in the yard with me,* she heard God say. Outside, trees were in their summer green.

Green?

'Why, green wasn't a single colour! I counted eleven separate shades that till that moment I'd simply called "green".'

And if the physical world was glorious, the spiritual one was more so! It was a visitor to her hospital room, an elderly man she scarcely knew, who introduced Molly to a world even closer than her own backyard. The old man stood at the foot of her bed and wept. She couldn't ask him what the trouble was because of the tube down her throat, so she asked God. And God said,

He's crying because he loves you.

'But I've never done anything for him!'

He loves you because you are lovable.

Lovable? Just . . . by being? Just . . . lying in a hospital bed accomplishing nothing? For Molly that old man's tear-streaked face was her burning bush. 'All my life I'd tried so hard to earn love – starting with God's. I was taught as a child that if you were good enough, you'd go to heaven when you died. Now I know it's not a question of how good I am, but how much God loves me. Why, I'm in heaven right now!'

Molly knew she was dying, and she knew she didn't have to wait till then to enter Paradise.

The Prison Yard

The tree which moves some to tears of joy is in the eyes of others only a green thing which stands in the way.

William Blake

Like Molly, the British novelist Philip Toynbee began to see only after he was diagnosed with cancer. 'I stopped several times,' he wrote in his journal after a walk, 'and looked at a single tree as I have never done in my life before. Intense happiness.'

A month before he died, he wrote, 'Wet leaves of sycamore after a heavy shower, and the sun glittering on them . . . Such things I now look at with renewed intensity and happiness – not because I may not see them for much longer, but because they are of immediate significance: almost direct manifestations of heavenly light.'

The sacred in the commonplace . . . Corrie ten Boom was another who 'took off her shoes'. Corrie could detect heaven in the grimmest places! In fact, the book John and I wrote with her, which we titled *The Hiding Place,* in some foreign editions was called *Heaven in Hell.*

Having experienced the depths of human brutality in a Nazi concentration camp, and having detected heaven even there, Corrie forever after looked for – and found – heaven wherever she was.

I went with her once to Scheveningen Prison in Holland, where she spent the first weeks after her arrest for the 'crime' of sheltering Jews. With liberation, Scheveningen had reverted to its pre-war function as a men's penitentiary, and Corrie was often invited there as a chapel speaker.

'I love talking to these men!' she said as we waited just inside the formidable gates of this maximum security facility. 'I tell them, the gates of this prison are locked and bolted, but the gate of heaven is open wide!'

Massive brick walls hemmed in the yard where we stood. With a little cry of delight Corrie pointed to a spot high above my head. A fragile-looking white flower had somehow thrust its roots between the bricks, somehow found moisture and nourishment as it stretched toward the sun. 'Oh, I must tell them about that! I must tell them that new life can burst even through prison walls!'

She shook her head wonderingly. 'How can people be so blind? Heaven is everywhere you look!'

The Blackboard

I'd like to see always like Molly, like Corrie. But glimpses of heaven come for me only sporadically. I look up from my word processor right now . . . Doubtless heaven is before my eyes, but all I see is a pile of unanswered letters and a window screen that needs replacing.

Like all people with poor natural vision, I'm familiar with the phenomenon of failing to see what's visible to others. I remember as a first grader going to the front of the music room after weeks in school and to my amazement discovering a blackboard. From my seat I'd mistaken the board for a dark wall. I stepped closer. A treble clef in white chalk! Staff lines, notes!

How, I wonder today, *could I have sat every Thursday in that room without suspecting that more was going on than I perceived?* The music teacher must have been writing on the board all along. The chalk must have squeaked. How could I have missed it?

And even having discovered the blackboard, it never occurred to me that I should be able to see it from my seat. To read what was on it, obviously, you walked up to it.

Mistaking one's limited vision for the whole picture . . . Today I know that we who are spiritually shortsighted do the same. If anyone had asked me, at age six, I would have said of course I could see everything in the music room! A blackboard in school, heaven here in my study. Right before my eyes. Unseen.

It wasn't till I was twelve that my poor eyesight was finally detected. How much longer I might have gone on, satisfied with my partial world, I don't know. But in the summer of 1940, our family travelled by car from New York to Los Angeles – a long trip on two-lane roads! Daddy had never forgotten the beauty of California as

111

he'd seen it in 1906; now at last the Schindler agency was to open a West Coast branch.

Somewhere on that long drive, he apparently noticed that I never commented on the scenery. We three children and the cocker spaniel shared the backseat of the big black Packard. I wrote in my travel diary, invented long hair-raising narratives to keep Donn and Caroline entertained, read *Jane Eyre* and *Wuthering Heights* – and never looked out the window.

Daddy began testing me. 'Read that sign up ahead.'

'What sign?'

As soon as we got to California, my father assured me, alarm in his voice, I'd go to an eye doctor. I couldn't understand his urgency. What you don't see you don't miss. . . .

It was Mother who took me to the optometrist in Los Angeles, then to an optician's to choose among uniformly hideous frames. Like most twelve-year-old girls, I was newly aware of my appearance. The past year in school I'd also become aware of boys. I wanted to know more about them, and as soon as some of them got as tall as I was, I was going to try.

Wearing *glasses* would spoil everything. No designer frames then! Glasses really were made of glass – heavy, thick, metal- or horn-framed, ugly. They could get me glasses, I decided, but they couldn't make me wear them.

In a few days the ominous things were ready. The optician fitted them, leaning across the counter, then slipped them into a brown leather case. 'Have her wear them around the house,' he said to Mother, 'until she gets used to them.'

As we walked to the car I took the bulky things from the case – Mother had picked the horn-rims – and slid them curiously over my nose. The next instant I almost fell backward. As stunning as a physical blow, the pavement sprang at me from the ground. I raised my head. People leaped toward me. Hard-edged buildings crowded close. Everything was nearer, brighter, firmer than it could possibly be.

It was a day or two, as the optician warned, before I could move confidently with my new vision, knowing I wouldn't bump into the objects rushing toward me. But there was another adjustment that took longer. Seeing the world as it looked when I took the glasses off. Indistinct rooms, blurry landscapes . . . had I really believed this was reality?

A pair of lenses, two slivers of glass, and the world came into focus for me. Fantasies of glamour forgotten, since age twelve I've reached for my glasses as I open my eyes in the morning, removed them only after switching off the light at night.

And did I really believe, all those years when I was unaware of the Way I walked, that this physical world was the whole of reality? Like the blackboard in a schoolroom, how impossible it seems to me now that I could have missed the obvious.

Seeing

The world will never starve for want of wonders, but only for want of wonder.

G. K. Chesterton

Seeing what's there, seeing heaven, starts with getting the focus right. But there's a second half. The mind must comprehend what the eyes take in.

The Los Angeles detective agency did not succeed. With too few clients in California and the New York office busier than ever, Daddy drove the family back east. And on the way we visited the Grand Canyon.

Daddy held out the promise of the three-day stopover there as a consolation – to Mother for a second huge packing chore in six months, to us children for another change of school. As we climbed into the Packard and drove away from the rented house in Westwood, he talked up the natural wonder awaiting us.

Listening, I formed a mental image of a steep-sided vertical cleft in the earth. As I imagined it, the Grand Canyon was about three feet across and bottomlessly deep. A slit in the ground plunging straight to the centre of the earth.

As we neared the lodge on the canyon rim, my heart hammered so hard it hurt. For hours we'd driven through a desert moonscape. Hills, valleys, multicoloured rock, barren and beautiful. Just the setting, it seemed to me, for the awesome phenomenon we were about to see.

'Here we are!' Daddy announced, pulling into the parking lot. We walked beneath some stunted pines to a rocky ledge overlooking the widest valley yet. Sculptured rock formations filled the space between the plateau where we stood and another plateau, miles away.

But . . . where was the Grand Canyon?

The mesas rising from the valley floor before us were rust and pink and tawny yellow, somewhat more varied than those we'd been driving past all day. Still, it was simply another western panorama, more scenery of the kind we'd been looking at. I mumbled something about going back to the car for my diary; I didn't want the others to see me cry.

If we had left then, if that afternoon had been the whole visit, this disappointment is all I would remember. But we spent two nights at the lodge. Next morning we followed a trail part of the way down, that afternoon drove to another vantage point on the rim. And slowly, little by little, hour by hour, I began to *see* the Grand Canyon.

Immense, overwhelming, vast beyond comprehension, it had simply been too big to take in all at once. This time it was not a question of optometry. With my new glasses, shape and colour, depth and breadth were perfectly visible. Seeing, in this case, meant, in part, letting go of a preconceived image – that three-foot-wide slit in the earth. And in part, letting mind and spirit expand to take in something grander than anything imaginable.

By the third day, as we walked to the rim for a final view of the Canyon, I was too filled with wonder to join in the family's enthusiastic appreciation. I felt tears rise again, fogging my glasses. 'I think you're coming down with something,' Mother said. 'You're sniffling and you haven't said a word about our lovely stay here.'

I had no words. Years later I would hear a phrase at the start of a church service: 'God is in his holy temple, let all the earth keep silence before him', and understand why I had been dumbstruck in that place.

The Signpost

> 'Help us to find God,' the disciples asked the elder. 'No one can help you do that,' the elder said. 'Why not?' the disciples asked amazed. 'For the same reason that no one can help fish to find the sea.'
>
> *Joan Chittister*

Why can't I see heaven around me today? Is it my nearsighted spiritual vision? Is it some preconceived notion about what heaven

114

should look like – an ethereal realm-in-the-sky, perhaps – so unlike the real thing that I fail to recognise it? Or . . . is heaven simply too close, too all-encompassing, for me to perceive?

I remember crossing the border into Spain after dark one November day. John and I had been driving south along the Atlantic coast of France since daybreak and were eager to reach the Spanish town of Fuenterrabia where our map showed the only 'lodging' symbol in the area.

On the map Fuenterrabia looked only a short way past the border, but mile after mile passed and we hadn't come to it. The only road sign our headlights picked out said 'Hondarribia' – too small a place, apparently, to be on the map. Finally John turned the car around. 'Let's go back to Hondarribia,' he said, 'and get directions.'

Hondarribia turned out to be a sizable place, evening rush hour in full frenzy. 'I'm surprised there's no hotel here!' I said.

On a traffic island we spotted a signpost, arrows pointing to town names in every direction. To a chorus of irate honking, we circled the island three times.

Fuenterrabia was not on the signpost.

For another quarter hour we wandered aimlessly through the congested streets, until at an intersection we spotted a policeman directing traffic. John stopped the car, bringing on a fresh outbreak of honking, while I rolled down the window.

'*Disculpe, senor,*' I brought out my meagre store of Spanish, 'we're trying to find Fuenterrabia.'

With a flourish of a white-sleeved arm, the officer set the traffic flowing around us and leaned down to the window.

'Fuenterrabia,' I repeated. 'We're looking for Fuenterrabia.'

A look I could not read came over the policeman's face. Anger? Sorrow? Lips pressed together as if to prevent a word escaping, he straightened up. Lifting his right arm, he stabbed his gloved forefinger with an emphatic gesture toward the ground at his feet. Once, twice, three times.

'Here?' I said. 'This is Fuenterrabia right here?'

A final vigorous stab and he turned back to the tangled traffic.

It was our introduction to the Basque separatist movement. 'Of course he wouldn't utter the word "Fuenterrabia,"' a friend in Madrid later explained. 'That's the Spanish name for the place. In Basque it's "Hondarribia".'

Not only did patriotic Basques refuse to speak Spanish, our friend said, they removed Spanish-language road signs as fast as the government could put them up. 'Spanish maps are no good in that area.'

In Fuenterrabia/Hondarribia, sure enough, we found a hotel room, sampled the delicious local octopus, and in the morning attended a church service packed – though it was only a Tuesday – with fishermen singing their full-throated Basque hymns.

But when I think of that city, it's a white-clad policeman I see, pointing at the ground where he stood. *This is the place. You're in it. You're already there.*

Why don't I see heaven? Perhaps because I'm looking for signs to somewhere else instead of examining the place where I am right now.

The Prayer Closet

The Church blesses some things, not because some things are holy and others are not, but so that we will know that everything is holy.

David M. Allen

I've been in heaven all along, I know now, only the signposts that could tell me where I was were written in another language. I thought heaven came when problems were behind me. But the signs, as I've learned to read them, say heaven lies right in the middle of them.

I remember, years ago, arriving at 7:00 in the morning at the California home of Roy Rogers and his wife, Dale Evans. This was the time in our family when seven-year-old Scott spent ten minutes before the mirror each morning adjusting his cowboy hat and six-shooters to match the photo of Roy on his wall. I'd come west with a Roy Rogers songbook and a dozen reminders from Scott to ask Roy to sign it.

It wasn't Roy I'd come to see, though. I was there to interview Dale on a subject seldom discussed in the 1950s: how to mix career and family – seven children in Dale's case! I wanted answers not merely as a reporter but for myself. I had only three children, and work I could do for the most part at home, but still felt tugged in many directions. Here at last was someone with experience.

I'd heard that strength for Dale's many-sided life came from daily prayer. When? I intended to ask. How did she ever find the time?

The door of the rambling ranch house was opened by a teenage girl. 'I can't find my gym shoes!' she wailed. As I stepped inside, a plastic airplane sailed past my knees, followed by a tow-headed boy in blue pyjamas. 'Mom's in the bathroom,' he said.

Dale had asked me to come at this early hour because she and Roy had a recording session later that morning. I found her dabbing a piece of cotton on the mouth of a sobbing five-year-old. 'Debbie cut her lip on the washstand,' she said. The little girl comforted, Dale looked at her watch and sprinted for the kitchen. While she cracked eggs into a bowl and fed slices of bread into a toaster, I poured orange juice into a row of glasses lining the counter.

'Sandy!' to the youngster in pyjamas, 'why aren't you dressed?'

'Because Dusty has my pants.'

And so it went as children appeared, ate, dashed out the door. It was like a whole week of crises at our house – the missing note for school, the juice spilled on the only clean shirt, the scuffle that the other one started. And in the midst of it all, Roy's voice from somewhere in the back of the house, where the phone had been ringing nonstop. 'It's the studio. Can we come an hour earlier?'

When the last child had been inspected, kissed, and waved to the bus stop, Dale sank with a sigh into a chair. It seemed a cruelty to press questions on her now, but . . . how in the world did she manage a prayer life? Did she have a place apart somewhere – someplace away from pressures?

Yes, she said. 'Come on, I'll show you.' She led me outside and around behind the barn. There, out of sight of the busy household, was a jumble of giant boulders honeycombed with hidden nooks. It was the hideaway of my childhood dreams. I could understand, I said a little enviously, how she'd feel close to God in such a setting.

'You'd think so, wouldn't you? But I never did.'

I had asked, she reminded me, if she *had* a place to escape to, not if she used it. 'At one time I did. I used to come out here a lot. I had the idea that prayer meant time apart.'

But sitting here among the silent rocks, she'd heard only her own spinning thoughts. *Why wasn't Linda eating? Was Dodie napping or getting into mischief?*

'Then of course, I'd feel guilty because I wasn't praying. God seemed a million miles away, and I knew it was my fault.'

117

Seeking answers, she'd joined a group of women on a three-day silent retreat at an Episcopal convent up in the mountains. In that serene and holy place God did indeed speak to her. And what he said was, *Don't look for me here. This is where I am for those I've called to be nuns. For you, I am in the noise and the bedlam and the peas on the floor.*

And that's where she'd found him, Dale said, ever since. We went back to the kitchen, where she showed me Scripture cards in a little loaf-shaped box. 'My "daily bread",' she said. Instead of waiting for that imaginary free hour when she could read the Bible, 'I need just a free second. While I wait for the cereal to boil I'll draw out a verse and memorise it.'

Prayer had become a constant thing, she went on, woven through the day's busyness – driving the car, waiting for a child at the dentist. 'Heaven, I've learned,' said Dale, 'is not up on that mountaintop or hidden away among the rocks. It's not me getting off to be with God, but God beside me every hour of every day.'

Light Show

> **In growing fields of corn,**
> **The lily and the thorn.**
> **The pleasant and forlorn,**
> **All declare God is there.**

> *Elder Hibard*

Heaven every hour. Even an hour of physical pain?

I think of another car trip, this one in Germany, when I was aware of existing in two seemingly incompatible worlds at once. It was five days before Christmas, 1973. Our college-age kids were flying over to join us for the holidays in Europe where John and I were working. Their flight was due in Luxembourg at 4:00 that afternoon.

And I woke up that morning in Munich, 300 miles away, pain stabbing my chest and arms, and a 104-degree fever. There was no postponing the drive to Luxembourg: The flight's arrival was our only contact point. 'We'll stop at the first town we come to after doctors' offices open,' John said.

He lowered the passenger seat of our rented Renault to almost flat and half carried me to the car in the predawn dark. Head throbbing, muscles burning, I felt every bump in the pavement, every turn of the wheels as he steered through the streets of the city and onto the highway.

And then the sun came up.

During the night, a freezing fog had settled over Germany. Every tree limb, every bare branch and twig, was wrapped in a sheath of ice. Lying nearly prone, the tops of the trees lining the autobahn were all I could see. But these were not shapes of wood and bark! They were trees of fire, dazzling diamond bursts of sheer colour. Overhead they passed, a never-ending stream of flashing rainbows . . . more colours than I knew existed . . . more splendour than my mind could grasp.

Hour after hour, mile after mile, the celestial ice show continued. John, eyes on the road and German drivers, could only steal glances at the glory erupting around us. But I lay bathed in it, feasting on light and beauty and joy.

And hurting. That was the mystifying thing about the experience. I was in as severe pain as I could almost ever recall, sick to my stomach, too, in the rocking car, physically miserable. And yet simultaneously, on a totally separate level, entranced, delighted, supremely happy.

We stopped in Augsburg, where a doctor diagnosed pneumonia and put me on medication that by evening had lowered the fever. But all that long day, two realities, misery and bliss, coexisted.

The Valley

> **All praise to Him who now hath turned**
> **my fears to joys, my sighs to song,**
> **my tears to smiles, my sad to glad.**
>
> *Anne Bradstreet*

Ever since that December day, I've looked at paintings of martyred saints – those scenes of fire and rack so favoured by medieval painters – with new understanding. The flames rise, the arrows pierce, the branding iron burns, and the saint gazes rapturously into heaven. 'Sorrowful, yet always rejoicing,' St Paul wrote to the church at Corinth about our life in two realities.

I wonder in fact if it isn't the painful times that bring heaven closest. I think of Molly Shelley, discovering God's love on a hospital bed. Corrie ten Boom finding heaven in the hell of a concentration camp. John seeing Jesus in an ICU. It's in the valleys, not on the peaks or the level stretches, that a light from heaven so often bursts on the path.

I know a man for whom it happened literally that way – a sudden, life-changing stab of light in a dark, dark night.

Max Ellerbusch was showing me around his comfortable home in Cincinnati. 'And this is Craig,' he said, lifting a photograph from the living-room table. A five-year-old boy with curly blonde hair and an irresistible grin smiled out at us from a silver frame.

This was the child who, on the Friday before Christmas eighteen months before my visit, had blown a good-bye kiss as he headed out the door for the last day of nursery before the holidays. At the school crossing, a block from home, he'd waited, as his father reminded him each morning, for the crossing-patrolman's signal. The car came so fast the patrolman had to jump backward to keep from being killed too. The driver never stopped.

'When they told me Craig was dead, I was plunged into a blackness I can't even describe,' Max said. His wife, Grace, was stunned with grief. But for Max it was more than grief. Raised in a loveless home, he'd seen little to be glad about until his own four children came along. Craig especially, with his infectious joy, seemed to say, 'It's a wonderful world!' And then . . .

'All the anger I'd carried from childhood focused on the driver of that car.'

Police made the arrest twenty-four hours after the accident. George Williams (not his real name), fifteen years old. His mother, raising him alone, worked a night shift. While she slept on Friday morning, George had cut school, taken his mother's car keys from her handbag . . .

Max spent Saturday on the phone – lawyers, police, newspapers – demanding that Williams be tried as an adult. 'I wanted to go to that jail and strangle the punk who'd killed our Craig.'

It was late Saturday evening, a day and a half after the tragedy, the blackest hour of the night, the blackest time of Max's cheerless life, when the lightning bolt from heaven fell. For a second sleepless night, Max was pacing the hall outside his bedroom, when . . . the dark little corridor was suddenly ablaze with light.

'Bright as the sun. Brighter! Brighter than any light on earth could be.'

And in that unearthly brilliance, Max's grief, his rage, his lifetime of bitterness, vanished like goblins imagined in the dark. 'It was pure love, that light – an overpowering, all-encompassing love that I knew had to be God. I knew in that instant that Craig was all right – better than all right! And I was all right, and everything, everywhere was all right.'

Everything except the future facing George Williams. In that same light-struck moment, Max saw a confused, lonely boy as much in need of a father as Max was of a son. He burst into the bedroom where Grace too was sleepless. Max's words tumbled over themselves. 'Christmas is coming. We can send presents. Go to the jail. Tell George we love him . . .'

And love him Max and Grace did. They asked for and got his release, and though at first George was afraid to meet them, the Ellerbusches' soon became his second home. After school he'd stop in to work with Max in his instrument repair shop or join the family for a meal around the kitchen table. George was there the afternoon of my visit, a gangly teenager with an outbreak of acne on his forehead, helping his 'little sister' with her homework.

I kept up with the Ellerbusches over the years, as George grew up and started a career and family of his own. But it wasn't just a fifteen-year-old's life that was transformed in that heaven-lit moment. The Max Ellerbusch I know is an outgoing person, demonstrative in his love for his wife and his children.

'That wasn't me at all,' he says. 'If you'd known me before this happened, you'd wonder, *What's bugging this guy?* I had a chip on my shoulder the size of a log.'

I have to take his word for it – and Grace confirms it. 'He was so uptight he'd grind his teeth in his sleep.'

And the transformation came, not when all was well, but in the deepest valley of his life.

They never last long, these flashes from heaven. Maybe here on earth we can't endure such brightness for more than an instant. One Sunday morning at St Andrew's Cathedral in Aberdeen, Scotland, in 1999, the opening hymn was about angels:

> They sing because thou art their Sun;
> Lord, send a beam on me;
> For where heaven is but once begun
> There alleluias be.

The author knows that light from heaven! I thought. John Mason knows that a single beam from that Sun will change a life. One ray, and we join the chorus that forever sings 'Alleluia!'

The Gift

It's *too* good, that's the trouble with the heaven to which Jesus the Way is taking us. It can't be true, the gift is too enormous, certainly it can't be meant for *me.*

In the inquirers' classes before my confirmation, I went through a sequence of emotions. Disbelief, dawning comprehension, joy. Jesus was *my* Truth, *my* Way, *my* Life?

Six months after my trip to the cathedral in June 1962, when I recited the Creed and was confirmed, I watched the same progression mirrored in the face of a small boy who likewise received an unimaginable gift. Tomu was the seven-year-old son of the yard man whose services came with the house we rented in Uganda that fall. All day Tomu trailed behind his father as he cut the grass with great swipes of his machete.

Tomu followed his father, that is, until the little boy heard a car coming. At the approach of an automobile – an infrequent occurrence on our isolated hilltop – Tomu would run to see it appear. He simply doted on cars; he could hear one coming moments before the cloud of red dust on the road below alerted me to an impending visit.

Often it was the green VW bug driven by the editor of the Kampala newspaper for which John and I were writing. As long as that car sat in our driveway, Tomu would hover near it, occasionally reaching out to touch it reverently with a single finger.

As Christmas approached, I went shopping in Kampala. And there I saw it, in the window of a toy store: a miniature VW eight inches long. And wonder of wonders, it was green!

When we gave Tomu his package on Christmas Eve, he made no attempt to open it. He turned the box in its red-and-gold wrapping over and over in evident fascination, then politely handed it back.

Nine-year-old Donn was Tomu's idol. Donn took the box, untied the ribbon, undid one end of the paper, and gave it to the little boy again. Tomu gazed admiringly at this new configuration and again handed it back. Taking off the rest of the gift wrap, Donn lifted up the box lid.

Seeing the toy car, Tomu's face reflected the kind of awe you see in paintings of saints confronted with the celestial vision. When he still didn't reach for the car, Donn lifted it out and handed it to him. The child held it on his two outstretched hands, trembling a little at being in contact with anything so glorious.

Then, solemnly, he handed it back once more.

I began to wonder whether this little boy had ever had a store-bought toy. 'Kapa! Kapa!' Donn kept telling him, Swahili for 'gift'. Tomu, however, spoke only the local Luganda language. Placing the toy car again in his hands, pointing to him, then to the car, then back to him, Donn at last communicated that he was to keep this object. That it was his. That he could take it away with him.

And then! Then I saw on Tomu's face a joy like the sunrise. Incredulous joy, celebratory joy, an open-mouthed smile that kept coming and wouldn't stop.

I recognised that joy. It was the joy I'd felt when slowly, stumblingly, uncomprehendingly, I grasped that inside the gorgeous packaging of St Mark's – the Gothic architecture, the splendid organ, the stately English of the Prayer Book – was the Gift itself. God's love, infinite, eternal. And that this love was mine.

No tiny part of it had I earned. I doubt if Tomu's family, in that almost cashless society, *could* have gone toy shopping. Tomu's gift, like mine, had to be purchased by someone able to pay the price.

My gift too had been paid for and held out to me. God's problem, as Donn's with Tomu, is to persuade the recipient that what is too good to be true *is* true, nonetheless.

The Nurse Who Cried

> Both heaven and hell are banquet halls,
> tables piled high with food. In hell, however,
> everyone is starving; the spoons are three
> feet long and people can't get the food to
> their mouths. In heaven the spoons are three
> feet long, too, but a great feast is underway.
> The diners feed one another.
>
> *Anonymous, 'The Two Banquets'*

We have our individual reasons for feeling that heaven cannot be meant for us. One of mine is my selfishness.

In the *Divine Comedy,* Dante set down the most elaborate conception of the afterworld ever written. So detailed are its descriptions of hell, purgatory, and heaven that many of his contemporaries in the fourteenth century believed he'd actually made the imaginary journey he describes.

In the *Inferno* Dante encounters the souls in hell. Though he meets a wide variety of people in its gloomy landscapes, all have one quality in common. Each one believes himself the centre of the universe. In each of hell's nine circles, the damned assail Dante with their ongoing feuds, their self-justifying accounts of what went wrong. Nothing exists outside their thwarted desires, their wounded pride. It's chilling reading!

August, 1968. It was Liz's turn to go with me on an interview trip, but as the two of us set out in the car for Springfield, Pennsylvania, I had misgivings. How would a twelve-year-old react to meeting Dick Riley?

'Of course, bring your daughter along!' Mr Riley had said over the phone. Still, Liz was a child who wept over limping dogs. And from what I'd heard about Dick Riley . . . 'You mustn't be alarmed when you see him,' I tried to prepare her.

Sixteen years earlier, in a fall from a ladder, the man we were going to see had been paralysed from the neck down. Years of rehab had restored partial use of one arm so that with this crippled arm he could shift himself in bed. His lifeless legs had been amputated. 'You mustn't stare,' I told Liz. 'Or act sorry for him.'

Dick Riley's wife, Mary, welcomed us at the door and led us to the room where Dick was propped on pillows in a motorised bed, surrounded by the files of his accountancy business. On that summer afternoon a sheet was the only bed covering, too smooth, too flat, where his body ended abruptly at his hips.

Mary brought us all ice tea, then took Liz out to the garden while Dick told me his story. He'd been only twenty when the accident happened, married, with a baby on the way. The house painting firm he was working for had assigned him a three-storey home that week.

'I was foreman on the job, bossing men twice my age.'

In the front of the house was a single small window high up. The company rule for third-storey work was one man up, one to hold the ladder, but that would mean calling one of his crew off the job at the back of the house.

What was one dinky window! 'I was Mr Independence.' Dick raised the extension ladder and scrambled up. With his putty knife he loosened one corner of the window screen, then reached for the other. He saw the side of the house slide past his eyes, heard the ladder slam to the ground a second before he did. He tried to stand up. He saw his hand six inches from his face. He tried to move it. . . .

The other workmen, hearing the crash, came running from the back of the house. At the hospital, doctors gave Dick only hours to live. Mary came, and the minister who'd married them and in whose church, two years earlier, Dick had accepted Christ. Together they thanked God that this very day Dick would be with Jesus in heaven.

But the hours stretched into days, then weeks, and Dick did not die. 'It was worse than death. I was a living person trapped in a corpse.'

The only thing he could still do was talk. And talk he did, aggressively, outrageously, trying to provoke anger, argument, anything to prove to himself that he could still impact his world. The hospital nurses were 'clumsy', 'stupid', 'lazy'. But instead of hot retorts, he received only kindness. He redoubled his attacks. If independence was the best word he knew, pity was the worst.

The point of his greatest despair, he told me, came when it was clear that, instead of dying, he might live on in this condition for many years. 'Instead of the fall sending me to heaven, it had landed me in hell.'

And like the denizens of Dante's hell, Dick's sole preoccupation was himself. He hadn't even noticed the face of the young nurse labouring over him one morning, struggling to get the sheet out from under him and get him turned. 'Of course she was doing everything wrong, and I was telling her so.'

And then . . . he became aware of another sound in that room. A strange sound in that space filled to overflowing with Dick's problems, Dick's needs. 'It was the very first sound I'd heard – really heard – since the accident.'

The nurse was crying.

Dick listened, staring at the wall he faced when turned on his side. He could not turn his head to see her. But looking at the wall, he was suddenly aware of her as a person. He pictured her setting out for the hospital that morning, leaving behind her own problems to take on a particularly disagreeable patient. He thought about the physical strain of the job, heard the carping cruelty he was adding to it. And he said, 'I'm sorry.'

Just two words. But they were the passwords out of hell. For a moment Dick had felt concern for someone else. Other moments followed. One by one he got to know the hospital staff. The birth of his son, Dicky, enlarged his world still more.

Then his employer's insurance ran out and Dick was moved from a private room into a ward. All around him were the needs of other people. He still lay paralysed in an unresponding body, but no longer in the prison of self. Motionless as he was, Dick found something to give each of his fellow patients. A joke. A smile. A prayer. A listening ear.

'You know who Jesus says goes to heaven?' Dick said. 'The guy who reaches out to the sick, the hungry. I can't find a single word in the Bible about independence.'

Dick continued reaching out. First in the rehab centre, today with family, friends and clients. 'The more I can give to someone else, the more God can give to me. His joy, that's what Mary and I know, every day of our lives.'

Dick didn't have to die, I thought, *to enter heaven.* Mary and Liz came in with flowers from the yard. When he learned that Liz would be starting junior high in a couple of weeks, Dick asked what he could pray for. Sixteen-year-old Dicky came in from a baseball game, and his dad demanded an innings-by-innings replay.

'Do you know what strikes me about your experience?' I told Dick as we got up to leave. 'It's *when* you found this joy.' I was remembering Max Ellerbusch, pacing the floor after little Craig was killed. 'It was when you heard somebody cry.'

Loss. Injury. Tears. Unlikely doorways to heaven, yet there was no mistaking where Dick Riley made his home. 'Mom,' said Liz as we headed home along the Pennsylvania Turnpike, 'what did you mean about Mr Riley? What was so awful? I mean, I saw about his legs and everything, but gosh, why would anyone feel sorry for him?'

The Sandwich Board

A whole man, an undamaged man, that was the person Liz and I met there in Springfield. Whole because Dick Riley's capacity for caring was intact. 'This is my commandment,' Jesus says, 'that you love one another' (John 15:12 RSV). This is the common currency of heaven.

For some, this *agape* love is as natural as breathing. I'm married to one of them. One of his mother's favourite stories was about the day John, aged six, asked her to do the lettering for a sandwich board he'd constructed. The wording on both chest and back, he instructed, was to be the same:

THIS BOY HELPS PEOPLE.

For weeks, his mother recalled, John walked up and down the pavement, displaying this announcement and performing small services for obliging neighbours.

This boy still helps people – friends, casual acquaintances, total strangers. A stranger, to John, is a friend he hasn't met yet. I'll leave our table at a restaurant in some town where we've never been, be gone five minutes, and come back to find another chair pulled up, John and a 'really interesting guy' in rapt conversation.

My father, though he'd have denied it, was another lover of people. He saw himself as a hard-boiled New York detective, inured to sad stories. Beggars' tales in particular. 'Dropping money in a cup won't help anyone. Give someone a handout, you make him an emotional cripple.' Yet he was incapable of passing a beggar without reaching into his pocket.

There was a bag lady whose chosen corner was Vanderbilt Avenue and 43rd Street, a block from his office. How Daddy discovered that her shoe size was the same as mine I never knew. Scarves, sweaters, mittens, all of us in the family were accustomed to see these appropriated for 'someone who needs this'. But shoes! I had to hide my cherished pair of loafers from Daddy's sudden raids on behalf of a charity he didn't know he possessed.

But what if we don't possess it? What if, like me, a person is not instinctively outgoing? I don't have the unconscious generosity of my father. John's undiscriminating goodwill toward everyone he meets. How can I accept the gift of heaven, unequipped to live there?

Joe

It was to Joe Bishop, that most loving man, that I took this question. In his study at the Presbyterian church he pastored in Rye, New York, I confessed my lifelong pattern of pulling away from people. When I wanted a break from the typewriter, I told him, I'd head off on my own. Drive to a bird sanctuary. Go to a museum.

'I don't ask anyone else along. Just do my own selfish thing.'

What puzzled me, I went on, was that I had friends I loved doing things with. Why did I need to be by myself when I could have a great time with others and give them pleasure too? 'I've tried and tried to change, but I can't seem to.'

'And why,' asked Joe, 'do you want to change?'

Well, because . . . wasn't it obvious? 'It's not loving! Look at John. Look at you.'

'But we're looking at you, Tib. Do you think when God created you, he meant to make someone else?'

Joe had known me for many years, he reminded me. 'I observed long ago that solitude is as necessary for you, Tib, as food and drink. Why not thank God for feeding you in this way?'

The withdrawing, the closed door that I'd struggled against all my life, was . . . okay? God-given, in fact? It was one of those heaven-tinged moments when in the mirror of someone else's eyes we catch sight of a better self than we knew.

I was in fact, Joe insisted, a profound lover of people – 'in your way, not John's or mine'. Me? Whose self-image was of a stand-offish person – *I* cared deeply for others?

Like Dad Sherrill seeing a beauty that came from himself, Joe's portrait of me, I suspect, was largely a projection of his own nature.

But that too is a hint of heaven! Perhaps God too sees us through the lens of his character, not ours.

I knew only, that day as I left Joe's study, that I was holding one of the keys to the kingdom of heaven. The lock does not open to prayer or good deeds or any other effort of our own.

The key is self-acceptance.

I can accept myself – delight in myself – because I am God's creation. It's a message I still have difficulty absorbing. Maybe its full impact must wait for the heaven that lies before us. But since that day in Joe's study, I've known that we cannot walk this Way at anyone else's pace, in anyone else's style, no matter how admirable. We can enter heaven only as ourselves.

Breakfast at Jean's

Why else were individuals created but that God, loving all infinitely, should love each differently.

C. S. Lewis

I know many Christians who've struggled, as I have, with this issue of self-love. It seems to run directly counter to Jesus' teaching! Aren't we to '*give up ourselves* to God's service', as the Prayer Book puts it? Aren't we to leave behind our 'old man', be conformed to Christ's likeness instead?

There came a time, some twenty years after John and I became believers, that we began to feel curiously isolated. For a while after our conversions, we'd savoured a wondrous new phenomenon. Community! After being onlookers at the Christian scene for years, we were now participants. It was a thrilling experience to meet a stranger's eyes and know, without a word being said, that he knew the God we knew.

For nearly ten years a small group of Christians met weekly in our living room. We didn't organise it – people simply showed up, new ones appearing, others departing in our very mobile suburb. Baptists, Methodists, Roman Catholics, a dozen denominations in my first-ever experience of a group in which I didn't have to be the leader or the reporter or wear any other disguise. I'd never imagined such vulnerability in a gathering of people! Or such depth of caring, as we prayed each other through tragedies and triumphs.

The bonding has remained, over time and distance, with each of these individuals. But not the sense of unity. Less and less were we encountering fellow Christians whose emphasis was our own. Always lots to admire, lots to learn from, but no longer any group with which we identified.

At last we decided to bring up the matter with the rector of St Paul's Church on Nantucket Island where friends lend us their home each spring. St Paul's is a turn-of-the-century Romanesque-revival building, as out of place among the prim wooden structures of that old Quaker whaling port as we were feeling in gatherings of Christians.

In its interior design, though, St Paul's is all Nantucket. My favourite part of the church is the small side chapel where stained glass windows celebrate whales and gulls, and needlepoint cushions portray a lighthouse or a sandy track through the moors.

In this evocative chapel each morning of the week, the Reverend Herbert Stevens held a service of Holy Communion. Afterward, Herb would occasionally be free to have breakfast with us. Breakfast with him meant Jean's, a no-frills restaurant on the outskirts of town. In the historic centre, where streets are cobbled with English stones brought as ballast in whaling ships, are some fresh-flowers-and-tablecloths breakfast places. Herb would have none of them: 'They're for summer people.' His chosen friends were the farmers and policemen and schoolteachers making a precarious living on the island year-round.

And so we'd drive out to Jean's, park among the pickup trucks, walk past the stools at the counter, and sit at a formica-topped table. John and I would sit, that is. It took Herb a long time to exchange news and greetings with fellow regulars. At last he'd remember that he had a breakfast date with off-islanders, join us at the table, and light a cigarette.

It was across the ketchup bottle at Jean's one morning that we brought up the isolation we were feeling. 'It's not that our faith means any less to us,' John said. 'Speaking for myself, it's never meant more.'

I nodded agreement.

'It's just that in groups of Christians,' John went on, 'we feel like outsiders. I guess the word for us is *lonely*.'

Herb signalled the waitress with his empty coffee mug. 'John,' he said, 'if you told me anything else, I'd be worried about you.

'Don't you know,' he went on, 'that each Christian life has its own pattern, different from any other? The longer we walk with God, the more closely we conform to the blueprint he's laid out for us alone, and the less like anyone else we become.'

The fried eggs arrived.

'The only problem I have with what you say,' Herb said, 'is the word you used. You don't have the right one at all. I don't see you as lonely, John and Tib. I see you as unique.'

Unique

What a freedom-giving word! Freedom to stop comparing our pilgrim's progress with anyone else's. Freedom to delight in reports of other journeys without devaluing our own or trying to make someone else walk our way.

Like most truths, it was so obvious, once spoken, that we wondered how we'd missed it. God who courts each of us so individually – who made a churchful of people icily aloof one September Sunday because a couple in the last row needed this – will he then turn around and blot out the differences he seemed to respect? Is the respect merely a ploy to get us through the door, behind which a divine cookie cutter goes to work turning out identical little Christians?

Of course not. Yet this was precisely the image I'd had, growing up outside that door. All Christians, I'd believed, though I didn't actually know any, were alike. What a releasing thing it's been, since that breakfast at Jean's, to recognise that the Christian walk means just the opposite!

The longer the walk, the more our individuality emerges. Longtime Christians in fact are the least conforming people I know! For God, who doesn't make duplicates even of snowflakes, is filling his heaven with millions upon millions of unique creations.

Entrance Exam

Herb Stevens' word *unique* resolved for me that seeming contradiction: do I 'love myself' or 'give myself up'? During a recent retreat at St Cuthbert's in Brewster, New York, I heard an old story from Eastern Europe that put it in four words.

Zuysa was the village rabbi, wise, kind, and beloved, who worried nonetheless that he might have failed to observe some commandment. He went to a mountaintop to ask God what more he needed to do.

'At the gate of heaven, Zuysa,' he heard God answer, 'I won't ask why you didn't give more to the poor, or fast more often, or memorise more Scripture. I will ask only one question.

'Why weren't you Zuysa?'

Why weren't you Herb . . . Molly . . . Corrie . . . Tib? Why didn't you show forth the aspect of God you alone embodied?

Zuysa's story was in my mind that night as I reread Paul's letter to the Ephesians. When he urges them to reach *'the whole measure of the fullness of Christ'* he can't be suggesting that anyone can do this solo! Paul was addressing Christ's Body, that Body with 'many members', no two alike. Each member with its special role, its part in the fullness of Christ that no one else can supply.

'Giving up myself,' I believe today, means giving up *my* notion of what my role should be and accepting – with joy – the one for which I was created.

To love myself is to accept God's evaluation instead of my own. And what a staggering value he places on each of us! In December 2000 I heard an Advent sermon in London's Westminster Abbey. The topic was sin. The fact is, said the Reverend Robert Wright, that 'I am as loved and worthy of esteem as I ever shall be – already infinitely loved and respected.

'The condition of not knowing this,' he continued, 'is sin. The tears that flow following its discovery are called repentance, in which we weep for the sin of ever having thought of ourselves as unloved, for not having loved ourselves as we are.'

Infinitely loved . . . as I am! Not as I will be, or could be, or might have been, but just the way I am this minute. To think less of myself is not humility but the pride that says I know better than God.

Bluebells

God loves each one of us as if there were only one of us.

St Augustine

How long has God been preparing each of us for that part no one else can play?

When I applied for confirmation at the Cathedral of St John the Divine back in 1962, the first question on the candidate form was *Date of Baptism*. I couldn't remember what I'd told the registrar of marriage banns in Geneva fifteen years earlier. In any case, it was a made-up date; I doubted such a ceremony had ever taken place. But when I telephoned my mother to ask, she surprised me. 'Why . . . yes,' she said after a moment's thought. 'It happens that you were.'

I was born, I'd known, in Los Angeles, during an earlier effort of Daddy's to open an office in his beloved California – as short-lived a venture as the one when I was twelve.

'There was the nicest man in the apartment next to ours in Hollywood,' Mother went on. 'He was a minister, so helpful, in a new place with a new baby.' He kept asking, she said, when they planned to have me baptised.

'He was so kind, and it seemed to mean so much to him. So one morning we went to his church, and he did a lovely little service. It was an Episcopalian church, I remember. Such a pretty garden out front.'

I put down the phone, absurdly elated at the denominational mesh. I'd not only been baptised, but in the very church where I now wished to be confirmed! The baptism of course would have been equally valid wherever performed. The coincidence was simply a little gift along the Way, like the bluebells planted beside Texas highways. *I planned your path from the beginning*.

What is confirmed in confirmation are the promises made on a child's behalf in infant baptism. That night I got out the *Book of Common Prayer* and read the Order for Baptism.

Do you turn to Jesus Christ and accept him as your Saviour?
I do.
Do you put your whole trust in his grace and love?
I do.
Do you promise to follow and obey him as your Lord?
I do.

I do. I do. I do. Promises made for me long before I could promise anything.

The Corridor

Turn to me and be saved.

Isaiah 45:22

It was not, however, the service in the cathedral with its solemn affirmation of baptismal vows that confirmed to me my new life in Christ – that life in heaven begun here on earth. That confirmation came in a casual conversation at *Guideposts'* office a few years later.

A friend from out of town, Jean Stone, had come to New York with a story suggestion. We talked it over, then she looked at her watch. 'I have a train to catch.'

'I'll walk you to the elevator,' I said.

We stood in the corridor, making conversation. 'Have you been saved, Tib?' she asked. The same politely interested tone in which she'd just asked how the children were.

And for the very first time in my life, I heard the question.

Jean Stone is a mannerly, soft-spoken person. As she quietly posed the question, I didn't hear a formula. Didn't hear judgement or an agenda being pushed.

I heard *saved* as a dictionary definition gave it when I looked it up later that day: *to guard intact.* As Jean said the phrase that had once made me too angry to listen, it was an inclusive, not a divisive one. My name on a place card at a glorious feast. I heard the word *saved,* and it sounded like *loved.*

'Yes!' I said as the elevator arrived. 'Yes, I have!'

Jean left. I walked back to my desk. My feet walked, that is, but my soul was dancing, turning cartwheels in heaven. Cherished, valued, guarded, whatever came, now and forever.

HEAVEN BEFORE ME

Rejoice that your names are written in heaven.

Luke 10:20

And even thou, most gentle death,
Waiting to hush our final breath,
O praise him!
You lead back home the child of God,
For Christ our Lord that way has trod.

St Francis of Assisi

'All the way to heaven is heaven,' St Catherine declared, and looking back on my journey, I've found it to be so. *Heaven behind me* – before I thought about such things at all. *Heaven around me* – the growing awareness of a larger reality. But *Heaven before me?* What can I know, this side of death, about the journey's culmination?

I can study the Bible. Ponder the insights of saints past and present. Recall my own intimations of that larger world.

As I've done all this, have I found answers that satisfy me? A few. But more than individual answers, what I've gained is the conviction that the life begun in heaven here, continues there. Wider, fuller, brighter even than our hopes.

The Basement

How differently I once thought of death! You died and that was the end of it. Belief in an afterlife was mere self-delusion. My introduction to the foolish notion had come not in church, but in the basement of the Louvre Museum.

I remember roaming its dimly lit corridors, peering at four-thousand-year-old mummy cases and wishing that, of all the subjects I could have chosen to study in Paris in the autumn of 1949, I hadn't picked Burial Objects of Old Kingdom Egypt. I'd been learning, in a French history course, about Napoleon's expedition to Egypt. Thanks to Napoleon, the instructor said, the Louvre had the greatest collection of Egyptian antiquities outside Cairo.

But when I'd enrolled at the School of the Louvre to explore these treasures, I'd discovered that the museum's classes were all for specialists. 'Burial Objects' – of the catalogue listings the one that sounded most general – consisted of an analysis of the probable original burial site of a certain alabaster jar, and a demonstration that the third leg of an acacia-wood stool had been repaired in antiquity.

So having paid my tuition, I wandered wistfully among the acres of unlabelled exhibits – this was long before the installation of today's user-friendly Egyptian wing. Every now and then I'd come upon a white-bearded classmate musing over the inscription on a sarcophagus lid. I was not only the sole female taking this course and the youngest by decades, but apparently the only one who did not read hieroglyphs.

To receive course credit, each student had to write a paper based on an original piece of research. My project, I decided, would be to determine whether the dozens of sphinxes lining the walls all curled their tails to the right.

Yes.

It was far too simple an observation even to think of submitting to the eminent Egyptologist at whose arrival in the lecture room all rose reverently. But my survey of sphinx tails led to the same discovery about the other artifacts in those basement rooms. These were standardised products. They were not art objects; the goal was not originality. The beautiful things placed in and around Egyptian tombs were tools for use in the next world.

It was my introduction, as I say, to the preposterous belief in life beyond the grave. And such unquestioning belief! Here was a brilliant civilisation devoting the lion's share of its energy and wealth to preparations for a mythical afterworld!

Armed with books on ancient Egypt from the nearby stalls along the Seine, I continued my solitary explorations in the Louvre basement. Egyptians, it seemed, could prepare so minutely for the next world because it was going to be just like this one. Only, of course, requiring longer-lasting materials. One book showed photographs of the huge step pyramid at Saqqâra, not only the largest building ever erected up to that time, but the first one made of stone. All around it, in an immense stone city of the dead, were offices, storehouses, stables, workshops, temples, officials' dwellings. It was an exact replica, on a far vaster, more permanent scale, of the merely temporary mud-brick city of the living nearby.

The more I read, the more the subject of an afterworld took on the appeal of a fairy tale; over the next few years, I traced quaint ideas about it through many cultures. What a universal idea life after death apparently was! Universal, too, to place it in an earthlike setting. From our hunting ancestors who buried their dead with bows and arrows, to the Chinese emperor interred with an army of life-sized clay soldiers, the afterlife was to be a continuation of this one.

People took along their horses, dogs, servants, wives – often killing them for the purpose. They brought food and cooking pots. The ancient Greek took a coin for the boatman who would ferry him across the River Styx.

If one's deeds in this life were good, the next life was conceived as pleasant. For Native Americans, the Happy Hunting Ground. For Greeks and Romans, an endless banquet. It would be the world they knew, minus its negatives. To the desert dweller, paradise was a watered garden. To the Norse warrior, Valhalla offered glorious battles with wounds that healed overnight.

Studying myths of the afterworld became for me a kind of hobby.

The Surprise

O God, you have prepared for those who love you such good things as surpass our understanding.

Book of Common Prayer

A decade after my wanderings in the Louvre basement, I began for the first time to read the Bible. And there I encountered the New Testament's view of the afterlife. Not yet a believer, I took its references to a 'kingdom of heaven' no more seriously than other ancient ideas about a blissful life-to-come. Here were the usual worldly pleasures. Like the rest of the Roman world, Christians looked forward to a never-ending banquet – the 'wedding feast' of the Lamb. Here were the negatives overcome: For the persecuted early church, heaven would have stout walls.

But then I noticed something else. Something different. Alongside the typical earthly imagery was a concept of the afterworld unlike that of any other tradition.

This world will surprise us!

It will not be what we think. Not what we *can* think. It will be another order of experience altogether. We can't come at such things, said St Paul, by earthly extension at all:

No eye has seen,
  no ear has heard,
no mind has conceived
  what God has prepared for those who love him.

1 Corinthians 2:9

Surprise had been the hallmark of every step of my Christian walk, and surprise – this idea of heaven as the utterly unexpected – was the first hint to me that it might, after all, be real.

Therese Martin, the French girl who died in 1897 at age twenty-four, spent much of her short life thinking about heaven. John and I have often stayed in the small provincial city of Lisieux where the girl often called 'the greatest saint of modern times' grew up in an ordinary-looking middle-class home still standing not far from the enclosed convent she entered, never to leave again, at age fifteen.

In her joyous anticipation of the life to come, only one thing worried Therese. Because she'd thought about heaven so much, she feared the reality would not be enough of a surprise. That God *wanted* to surprise her, she was certain. Hadn't he forbidden St Paul to reveal what he'd seen when he was 'caught up into paradise'? Hadn't he warned Paul that 'man may not utter' the glories there?

The next world was to be God's immense, joyful secret – and what if she'd guessed too much of it already?

'I've formed such a lofty idea of heaven,' she said as her tuberculosis advanced, 'that I wonder what God will do at my death to surprise me.' She would *pretend* to be surprised, she confided to her sister Pauline, even if she wasn't, so as not to disappoint him. It was God's delight, Therese believed, to astonish each of us, on our death, with the unimagined magnificence of his kingdom.

God of surprises . . . I was meeting him all through the Bible. A chosen people sprung from a barren woman past the age of childbearing. A holy nation founded by fleeing slaves. The King of kings born in a stable. Eternal life won by a hideous death. And heaven itself the greatest surprise of all.

The Anchor

We have this hope as an anchor for the soul.

Hebrews 6:19

Suppose, just suppose, I thought, *that this surprising heaven really exists!* All the 'primitive' age-old questions would be my questions too. Where is it? Who gets to go there? Will we know each other? Will we have bodies? What would we do with an eternity of days!

My first question, though, was whether there was any point in speculating about such things at all. If the real heaven is unknowable, God's well-kept secret, how can we form any idea of it? In fact, should we even try?

In the years since I wandered the dusty basement of the Louvre, I've come not only to believe in an afterworld, but to feel that we Christians *must* try to picture it. Not to mistake our human projections for the reality, as the Egyptians did. But to give us that hope that Christians have always described as the anchor of the soul.

In the sixteenth century a woman expressed her hope in a poem:

> O Master and Maker! my hope
> is in thee.
> My Jesus, dear Saviour! now set
> my soul free.
> From this my hard prison,
> my spirit uprisen,
> soars upward to thee.

The woman was Mary Stuart, Queen of Scots, awaiting execution in an English prison. Her serenity throughout her long ordeal, like that of Christians in every century, came from the hope of a better life to follow.

Faith. Hope. Charity. For a long time after I started going to church, I was puzzled by the inclusion of 'hope' in this great trilogy of Christian virtues. About Faith I heard many sermons. About Love even more. But scarcely a word about Hope.

Delighted at any excuse for research, I consulted the hefty theological tomes of various church libraries. Christian hope, it appeared, meant just one thing: the expectation of a glorious eternity in heaven. And for most of Christian history, it seemed to have been the *most* preached-about subject.

All very well, I thought, *in the past, when most people could hope for little on this earth.* Wasn't the historic emphasis on heaven simply escapism? Even, more ominously, a cynical ploy on the part of whatever group was on top – 'the opiate of the people', pie in the sky by and by? Weren't we right, nowadays, to downplay another existence? Hadn't focusing on heaven meant neglecting real needs here on earth?

No, thought C. S. Lewis. 'It is since Christians have largely ceased to think of the other world,' he writes, 'that they have become so ineffective in this.' From the deeds of a small group of apostles to the handful of English evangelicals who abolished the slave trade, 'all left their mark on Earth, precisely because their minds were occupied with Heaven.'

The Bullet

If we live, we live to the Lord; and if we die, we die to the Lord. So, whether we live or die, we belong to the Lord.

Romans 14:8

Reading Lewis's words, I thought of an interview John and I had had some ten years before. Martin Luther King Jr. was uppermost in my mind just then anyway: Three days earlier this thirty-nine-year-old Baptist pastor had been murdered as he stood on the balcony of a Memphis motel. Few men in our time, I thought, had left a greater mark on their corner of the earth than he had!

My overwhelming impression on meeting him, however, had been of a man 'occupied with heaven'. When John and I had arrived at his home in Montgomery, Alabama, in November 1958, he was recovering from a near-fatal stabbing. Two years earlier he had spearheaded a boycott of Montgomery's segregated buses, the first large-scale civil rights action in the twentieth century. Though his weapons were non-violence and love, a storm of hatred burst about him. Thirty or forty threatening phone calls and letters a day, his wife and baby daughter threatened, his home bombed.

For a full year, Dr King had refused to quit. When bus segregation ended in Montgomery, he wrote a book about the effectiveness of peaceful protest. He was in a department store in New York City, signing copies, when a deranged black woman plunged a razor-sharp letter opener deep into his chest.

By the time of our visit two months after the stabbing, he was allowed to leave his bed for meals, and he and Mrs King had invited us for lunch. Two memories of the meal stood out. The first was my introduction to collard greens, about which my kindest thought was that it must be an acquired taste. Since the end of the meal meant the end of the interview, however, I accepted a second helping . . . a third . . .

The other memory was the experience, equally new to me, of meeting a man who cared passionately about conditions in this world because his citizenship was in another. About passion for justice I'd learned from Grandfather, about a world beyond this one I had not. This was when heaven for me was still in the realm of myth; Dr King's lack of concern for his own safety seemed incomprehensible. He had no doubt, he told us, that in another place, on another street, in another town, the knife or the bomb or the bullet would find him. Meanwhile, he would not avoid public places, would not carry a gun, would not wear a bulletproof vest.

I looked at this twenty-nine-year-old man – a year younger than me – at his little daughter Yoki, just turned three, at thirteen-month-old Martin Luther King III, and wondered where such serenity came from.

As I followed Dr King's successful battles over the next ten years, I'd think of Grandfather's unavailing appeals for racial justice, of my own failed struggles at Northwestern, and wonder what his secret was.

'Like anybody else I'd like to live a long life,' he said in Memphis the night before he was shot. 'But I'm not concerned about that now. I just want to do God's will.'

That he was a fallible human being, he knew all too well. But that didn't concern him either. His hope was not in himself. 'I want to hear a voice saying to me one day,' he declared in that same fateful address on the eve of his assassination, '"I take you in and bless you because you tried."'

Apple Blossoms

We are . . . heirs, through hope, of thy everlasting kingdom.

Book of Common Prayer

For Dr King, the hope of being 'taken in' to a realm of eternal blessing was the anchor that held him steady. How I wish I'd been a believer when I had a chance to talk to him about heaven! How I'd like to have asked over the collard greens how he envisioned that future existence.

I didn't ask, though. All I'm sure of is that he did envisage it. Unknowable though the real heaven is, and far short as all human conceptions of it must fall, we cannot hope for something we can't imagine at all.

In November, 1972, a young man from a writing class I'd taught in Uganda came to New York on a journalism internship. Concerned about how Kiloto would handle the cold, I'd bought and borrowed a winter wardrobe for him.

But cold, it turned out, was not the problem. The problem was Kiloto's reaction to grey skies and bare-branched trees. Uganda is a land of year-round colour – vibrant flowers, jewel-like birds.

'I cannot remain in your country,' he would say. 'I cannot live in such a place.'

'This is temporary!' John and I kept telling him. 'Soon everything will be different. Trees will leaf out. Flowers will bloom.'

Kiloto could not conceive of such a transformation. Mental images of the beauty-to-be, so clear to us, were absent for him. Kiloto had never seen an apple tree in blossom. He went home in January.

No anchor held for him.

Hope needs images, needs to know about apple blossoms. I discovered this for myself a couple of years after Kiloto's experience when I visited my sister in Indonesia, where her husband worked with the Agricultural Development Council. Caroline and Alan had planned a wonderful car trip for me. 'The Puncak!' they told me excitedly. 'Imogiri! Yogyakarta! Ujung Pandang!'

I looked at them blankly. The unpronounceable names told me nothing.

Then we set out through the most beautiful countryside I'd ever seen. Temples, rice paddies, terraced green hillsides. At our first overnight stop, the bougainvillea at my window framed the symmetrical purple cone of a volcano. It was so breathtakingly lovely that I pleaded to stay on.

Caroline shut her suitcase and carried it to the car. 'You'll enjoy Borobudur even more,' she said.

I was sure I wouldn't. But of course that colossal ninth-century Buddhist temple rising from the plain like the many-levelled mountain of Dante's heaven is one of the vivid memories of my life.

And so it went at each stopover. Me hating to depart. 'Oh, do we have to leave?' Caroline and Alan practically dragging me away, to take me over my protests to a still more wondrous place.

I've wondered if the departure called death isn't a little like this. *Do I have to go so soon? Can't I stay just a while longer?* These places, these people, this beauty, I know. Of heaven I have formed no picture.

The Game

> **Breathe on me, breath of God,**
> **so shall I never die,**
> **but live with thee the perfect life**
> **of thine eternity.**

Edwin Hatch

Remembering me in Indonesia, Kiloto in New York, John and I often play a little game: describing to one another the 'perfect life' of heaven as we envisage it. Each person's image, of course, is different. I recall Ruth Graham's children asking, after a beloved dog died, if their pet was now in heaven. Instead of smiling at the question, Ruth went to the Bible. Heaven, she concluded from her Scripture search, is where each of us will be totally happy. And if someone's happiness depends on finding a particular animal there, then yes, heaven might well house dogs – horses, cats, canaries.

For someone else, happiness might require dance, or music, or a garden to tend. For Len LeSourd, heaven had to have meaningful work. In the last decade of his life, Len collected everything he could find in print about the next world. 'I don't think we'll just float about praising God on our harps,' he'd say.

He believed praise would indeed be unending, but also that God would have jobs for us. Among his papers, after his death, I found this paragraph:

Humans go to heaven as elected persons but flawed spirits. Broken relationships that aren't dealt with here have to be healed there. The immature who haven't grown up here, have to do so up there. Many mature spirits are trained to teach the immature. The teaching process is widespread and endless.

How Len looked forward to attending classes taught by St Paul! 'After that I'd love to be trained to teach a class of spiritual beginners. What a way to serve!'

He believed our work on earth prepared us for work we would continue to do in heaven. An editor in his earthly life, he joked about landing a job on the *Heavenly Gazette.* He admitted that communication in the next world won't require editing. But he was very serious in believing that God will go on using the gifts he's given us – more fully, more perfectly, than ever before.

For Len, heaven meant service. For John, who sings in St Mark's choir, it includes chorales led by a brilliant but tolerant conductor. Isabella d'Este, patron of Renaissance artists, was wealthy enough to build an earthly model of *her* celestial vision. In her *paradiso,* she surrounded herself with paintings, carvings, books, tapestries, cameos. Today in her five-hundred-room palace in Mantua, there's not much left of her paradise; her treasures are scattered through the museums of the world. But enough remains to glimpse heaven through the eyes of a lover of beauty.

What's in my own heaven? Lecture halls and libraries! An eternal schoolroom where I can study literature, botany, history, astronomy – all the fascinating subjects a single lifetime can't begin to explore. 'Are you *sure,*' I quiz John when we play our heaven game, 'that I won't wake up in the next world suddenly knowing everything?' For me the process of discovery is part of the joy. And John assures me solemnly that I will arrive with my ignorance intact.

The Icon

Is it only idle daydreaming, this designing of a heaven to suit our own taste? A self-indulgent fantasy; teasing ourselves with false hopes?

Or . . . is it possible that heaven is doing the designing?

On the wall in St Paul's Church on Nantucket is a small wooden panel with a painting of the church's namesake. St Paul is shown half length, his withdrawn, inward-looking eyes seemingly fixed on eternity.

I recognised it as an icon, those archaic, rather rigid devotional images of the Eastern Church, so I was surprised to learn that it was painted in the 1990s by the church's rector at that time, Andrew Foster. 'I didn't know you were an artist,' I told him.

'Oh, I'm not,' he said. Icons, he explained, are not 'art' in the Western sense. Self-expression has no more place in an icon than in Egyptian tomb crafts. The iconographer replicates as nearly as possible a hallowed image handed down from master to apprentice over the centuries. 'Icons are considered "windows into heaven". They're unsigned, dateless.'

I looked more closely at the portrait of St Paul. Bald, dark-skinned, curly black beard falling to his chest, he held in his hand a jewel-studded book. Around his head, glowing in the dim light of the sanctuary, was a metallic gold halo.

'Icons are different in another way,' Andrew went on. Western perspective, developed during the Renaissance, shows space receding away from the viewer, lines converging at a 'vanishing point' in the distance. In an icon, lines converge forward, meeting outside the painting, at the place where the spectator stands.

'It's not you looking at the painting,' said Andrew. 'The painting looks at you.'

The painting as the active agent, reaching out to include me in its celestial space. What if I've had it wrong, imagining with our heaven game that I am thinking about heaven. What if, instead, heaven is thinking about me?

The 'Hound of Heaven' pursuing us, as it pursued fleeing Jacob, planting a ladder at his feet as he slept. What if ours is always the passive role? Not us projecting our desires onto eternity, but eternity striving to imprint each of us with our true identity. Trying to mould each life into the unique pattern for which God created it. Preparing us for a world where all things fit together and each separate piece of the great design is essential to the whole.

Perhaps in the realm where past, present, and future are one, the design is already complete. Perhaps the Native American with his Happy Hunting Ground, the desert dweller with his garden, were not being naively literal, but catching whispers from eternity. Plato taught that everything on earth is merely a copy of its prototype in heaven. Perhaps a divine work assignment, an eternal choir, a heavenly art collection, an endless classroom, is tugging at different individuals here from a realm where these things have their full expression.

'Your soul has a curious shape,' wrote C. S. Lewis in *The Problem of Pain*, 'because it is . . . a key to unlock one of the doors in the house with many mansions. For it is not humanity in the abstract that is to be saved, but you – you the individual reader. . . . Your place in heaven will seem to be made for you and you alone, because you were made for it.'

Made for heaven. Made, through all the struggle, joy, suffering, and seeming chance of this brief earthly life, for an eternity of bliss no fantasising can equal.

Hope Chest

Our Creator would never have made such lovely days, and given us the deep hearts to enjoy them, above and beyond all thought, unless we were meant to be immortal.

Nathaniel Hawthorne

I think all of us are given foretastes of that bliss from time to time. I believe we should see them as very personal 'windows into heaven' and store them away in memory for those times when heaven seems farthest away.

When my mother's mother was growing up in South Dakota in the 1880s, she kept a hope chest. The 'chest' in Goggie's case was an old brown carpet bag. In it she placed a quilt, a lace doily, an embroidered pillowcase, beautiful things for the home she hoped one day to have. When snow blew for weeks across the prairies, or the wheat fields shrivelled in a summer drought, she'd draw the treasures from the chest and look beyond the discouraging present.

I never had a physical hope chest, but I keep a spiritual one now to aid me in cultivating the neglected virtue of hope. One of the treasures stored there is the graveside service following the funeral of my friend Molly Shelley. Molly could hardly wait for heaven! Having encountered God's love through the shades of green in her own backyard, she experienced it also in rain drops. Squirrels. People's faces. 'God couldn't love me enough to give me all this, if it wasn't to last!'

On my last visit to her home in Pennsylvania before her death from cancer at age forty-four, I found her stitching red and yellow felt balloons on a rectangle of blue cloth.

'My shroud!' she told me eagerly.

Balloons were to be the theme of her funeral. 'At the graveside everyone will have one. When they release them they'll soar up, up – way up till you can't see them anymore. But you'll know they're still there . . . flying free . . . just out of sight!'

Molly was bed-bound by then and in great pain; I had to take care not even to brush her mattress. Like Mary Stuart, I thought, when death released Molly 'from this my hard prison', she too would sing, 'my spirit soars upward to thee.'

Molly was also in emotional pain. Leaving a husband and six young children! Trying to prepare them for the grief she could not prevent and the future she could not share. But as we worked together on the funeral leaflet – with balloons, of course, on the cover – she couldn't hide her excitement at the still closer relationship awaiting her. 'Thank you for coming today,' began the letter from her that opened the service, 'to celebrate my returning home to our Father.'

Celebration. Release. Coming home. Previews of the joy to come are given us in many ways. For Molly it was the beauty of the 'commonplace' world around her. From her I learned to fill my hope chest with ordinary sights and sounds. Moments, for example, when the small routines of living seem to flow without effort – when I experience what our friend David Manuel calls a 'graced day'. The news item I wanted to hear is on the radio as I tune in. The person I've been trying to contact phones *me*. A car pulls out of the parking place as I drive up. It's a day when the timing of many schedules seems to mesh like notes in a symphony. When in the humblest event I 'catch the universe in the act of rhyming'.

My hope chest holds childhood memories, too. Like the Christmas when I was six and our family went to Florida by train. The view from the window was bleak as the Silver Meteor crossed New Jersey that mid-Depression year. Miles of rusting freight cars, grimy snow, rubbish-strewn tracks.

I woke in the morning puzzled for a sleepy moment by the jiggling of the berth. Then I was wide awake and staring openmouthed. In the night we'd entered another world. Pastel buildings, huge, slow-flapping pelicans, pinwheeling palms . . .

The dazzlement of that moment has never left me, and suggests what the astonishment at heaven will be, waking after sleep to find ourselves in a different land.

The Driveway

> **You were not created for Pleasure,**
> **you were created for Joy.**
>
> *Thomas Merton*

Among such 'everyday' memories, my hope chest holds one exceptional treasure. Why it should have been given me I've never understood, nor how to describe it.

It was a Friday afternoon in September 1967. For six days John and I and other staffers had been holding a workshop for the winners of *Guideposts'* first writers' contest. Seventeen men and women from all around the country had joined us at a conference centre in Rye, New York. Modelled after the French chateau where its owner was headquartered during World War I, Wainwright House has a book-lined library and green lawns sloping down to Long Island Sound. It had been the perfect setting for a week of interaction with some very talented people.

A few minutes earlier we'd waved our good-byes as the workshoppers departed. Now John and I too were going home, heading down the chateau's broad gravel drive, John at the wheel of the car. I leaned my head back against the seat, gazing at the first hint of autumn in the poplars lining the road at the end of the driveway.

And then, in the most vivid visual instant of my life, the scene in front of me broke apart. I no longer saw trees and a gravel drive. For an astonishing moment I seemed to be looking at the underlying substance of the universe.

The autumn light splintered into a billion shimmering fragments whirling in a kind of primordial dance. Even as I watched, I know I could not be seeing motion that fast – or particles that small. *Atoms are immense.* It wasn't a thought but an observation. Even parts of atoms – protons, electrons . . . *They're all too big to know about this.*

I was not only witnessing a scale unimaginably small and motion impossibly rapid, I was seeing a state of being unlike anything I knew. I was looking at laughter itself. I was seeing the fundamental structure of creation, and that structure was joy.

John turned down Stuyvesant Avenue, the vision ceased. A mile, two miles . . . 'Tired?' he broke the silence as he pulled onto Interstate 287.

No! Simply speechless, groping for a way to tell him what I could not possibly know and yet did know.

'Nothing exists,' I said finally, 'but joy.'

John turned to stare at me, then wrenched his attention back to the highway.

I described as best I could that momentary sighting of a reality beyond sight. It was knowledge, not emotion – to feel the joy I'd seen would have blown the human frame to bits. And the knowledge has stood unshaken, in all the ups and downs of all the years since, a kind of bedrock of certainty beneath all passing sensations. The base of everything, now and forever, is good beyond imagining.

Prayer Warrior

For this slight momentary affliction is preparing for us an eternal weight of glory beyond all comparison.

2 Corinthians 4:17 RSV

It was some years later that John and I stayed with our friends Michael and Jeanne Harper at an English retreat house near the site where Dame Julian of Norwich lived her self-imposed incarceration. And there I first encountered the writings of this fourteenth-century mystic.

Like her contemporary, St Catherine, whose footsteps I'd traced in Siena, Julian lived through the terrible years of the Hundred

Years' War. Catherine had confronted the evils of the day with outward action; Julian battled them with prayer, shutting herself away in a sealed cell attached to a church. Church and cell were destroyed by a bomb during World War II, but these were the fields, the hills, from which she'd shut herself off, to fast and intercede for a suffering world.

In *Showings,* that classic of Christian devotion, Julian recorded the revelations received in prayer. All are summed up in a single statement:

All shall be well, and all shall be well, and all manner of things shall be well.

Had Julian too, I wondered, seen the visible world break open to reveal the joy at its root? Is what, for me, was a fleeting one-time impression, for the saints a common experience? Even, for them, a constant perception, the insight that makes their lives of extraordinary endurance possible?

'The joy of the Lord is your strength,' Nehemiah told the Israelites, in what once seemed to me a poetic outburst. But maybe the man who rebuilt the walls of Jerusalem in the face of ridicule and plots against his life was simply reporting a fact. Perhaps when he looked at the 'hopelessly' ruined walls, he didn't see heaps of burned rubble. Perhaps he saw the joy vibrating beneath appearance and drew his strength from the sight.

Or when, as the writer of Hebrews tells us, Jesus endured the cross 'for the joy that was set before him' – perhaps the joy was literally before his eyes.

Superstring

Intimations of heaven! Like the lavender leaves my grandmother sprinkled in her hope chest, remembering keeps them fresh. That momentary sighting of a reality beyond sight, in the driveway at Wainwright House, remained so vivid over the decades that when I began reading about the superstring theory, it was with a shiver almost of recognition.

The theory, for a non-scientist like me, is bewilderingly complex, involving an unimaginable *nine*-dimensional universe. As George Johnson wrote in the *New York Times* in April 2000, 'Human brains are not wired to picture a world beyond the familiar three dimensions of space.' But picturable or not, physicists believe this may be the long-sought 'Unified Theory of Everything', from the smallest sub-atomic particle to the farthest galaxy.

What does the theory say this underlying reality is? Unthinkably tiny loops of threadlike material scientists have named, for lack of a better word, 'strings'. Entities so infinitesimal that, wrote Johnson, 'strings are to an atom as an atom is to the solar system'.

Yes! I thought, reading these words, *That small!*

The universe might be understood, the article continued, as a kind of mathematical music, a cosmic symphony 'played by an orchestra of tiny vibrating strings'.

I've witnessed that vibration, I thought.

Not comprehending, not even beginning to inquire into the physics. Simply joining for an enraptured instant in that universal dance. Catching a strain of the ecstatic music of heaven.

Maybe, I thought, there truly is a 'music of the spheres'. Maybe what I saw as motion, others perceive as sound – what Christians through the centuries have heard as the singing of angels. Our friend Carrol Maxwell heard them as she grieved for the death of evangelist Roy Hicks. Another friend, Ruth Prince, would hear angel song as she prayed. 'We realised,' her husband, Derek, wrote, 'that we were privileged to experience a tiny part of the total worship of the universe, spanning both heaven and earth.'

Worship. That's what it felt like, that day at Wainwright House. A taste of the eternal worship of heaven.

Becky

> And when this flesh and heart shall fail,
> and mortal life shall cease,
> I shall possess within the veil,
> a life of joy and peace.
>
> *John Newton, 'Amazing Grace'*

Once, fleetingly, I may have witnessed someone who was hearing the angels sing – another jewel for my hope chest. Becky was the six-month-old daughter of our friends Connie and Frank. I had volunteered to stay with her that evening so that Connie could attend Frank's company party given in his honour because he was being transferred that month to Michigan.

About 9:00, thinking the baby might have kicked her blanket off, I tiptoed into her room. To my surprise, Becky was wide awake, lying on her back. As I bent over her, she smiled.

Smiled? There's no word in the language for the expression I saw in the glow of the night-light. Her whole small being pulsed with a kind of ecstasy. The room seemed alight more with what shone from her face than from the pale little bulb in the wall. I'd often revelled in a baby's smile; this was a different phenomenon altogether.

This was joy itself.

In a moment or two, Becky's eyes closed, and a sweet sleeping infant was all I saw. And yet . . . for a little while, something not of this earth had been present in that room.

Frank and Connie moved shortly afterward, so it was not till nearly a year later than John and I learned of their tragedy. A month after they'd settled into their new home in Ann Arbor, Connie found their little Becky dead in her crib, a victim of sudden infant death syndrome.

It had taken eight months before they could write the letter 'To our friends'. All I could think, reading it, was, *I was given a glimpse of the joy Becky's sharing with saints and angels right now!*

I wrote back, trying to describe what I'd seen that night in her room. Whether it meant something to those grieving parents, I don't know. But forever after, the joy of heaven has had an infant's face for me.

Preparing for my confirmation a decade earlier, I'd memorised questions and answers from the catechism:

Q.   What do we mean by everlasting life?
A.   By everlasting life, we mean a new existence, in which we are united with all the people of God, in the joy of fully knowing and loving God and each other.

That was the joy, I believe, that I witnessed in Becky's smile. A split second of the everlasting life she lives today.

Park Bench

**Parting is all we know of heaven
– and all we need of hell.**

Emily Dickinson

But if Becky's death, for her, meant fuller life, for her parents, for all of us mourning a loved one, death means a terrible emptiness.

Some years ago, I sat on a bench in a waterside park in Singapore, watching primary school children performing acrobatics.

'My son,' the young woman next to me said shyly as a small boy scrambled to the top of a human pyramid.

A new group ran onto the field and my bench mate turned to chat. Though Singapore's population is Chinese, the official language is English. Where was I from? she asked. America. Did I have children? Three, I told her, all with families of their own. Which one did I live with? Not with any, I said. Then where did I live? Well, my husband and I lived in New York. Scott's family was in Nashville, Donn's in Miami, Liz's near Boston.

'Nashville . . . Miami . . .' she struggled with the unfamiliar names. 'Are they very near your street in New York?'

They weren't in New York at all, I explained. Liz wasn't too far, I went on, a five-hour drive. But Nashville was over a thousand miles away and Miami nearly fifteen hundred.

On the lawn, little girls were somersaulting over one another with wonderful precision. When I turned back to my companion, I was startled to see tears in her eyes.

'So far! So far!' she cried. 'Oh, when will they be back!'

Through this warm-hearted stranger I got a sudden look at modern American life as the anomaly it is in human history. I saw John and me forever packing suitcases for too-brief visits. Most family highlights – a son's music gig, a grandson's big baseball game – happening where we cannot be.

In tiny Singapore, where you can't go fifty miles without leaving the country, the generations live side by side in a pattern old as humanity. In our huge and restless country, the pattern is broken. I thought of my grandparents in Florida and California while I was growing up in New York. Thought of my own grandchildren's first steps, the first words, all of which I had missed. Thought of all the missing parts of ourselves, the empty, aching places a mobile society won't even let us acknowledge. And I too started to cry.

Passers-by may have wondered why a young Chinese woman and a middle-aged American were weeping, arms around each other, on a bench in a public park. But I knew. We were grieving for a sorrow as old as humanity. We were grieving for the ache of separation.

Death of course is the ultimate separation. The words we substitute for 'dead' say it nonetheless. Absent. Passed away. Departed. It's a departure so final that many cultures resist it, keeping the dead physically close, including them in the round of daily events.

One of the memorable times of my Indonesian trip was a visit to Tana Toraja. These mountain people on the island of Sulawesi bury their dead in niches carved high in the limestone cliffs. In one sheer rock face, Caroline, Alan and I counted a score of these alcoves. The height of a man, two feet deep, and as much as sixty feet long, they were fronted with wooden railings like balconies on a tall apartment building.

And the railings were lined with figures. Wooden effigies of the people interred in the hollowed-out rock behind, they stood shoulder to shoulder, twenty or more in a row, staring down at the living community below. Jewelled, turbaned, clothed in their best, keeping untiring vigil. It was the most haunting scene of the trip, that silent, watchful throng above us; though we knew they were only wooden carvings, we found ourselves speaking in whispers.

Periodically, relatives dress the effigies in new clothes. They bring them little gifts and ask their assistance with problems. In Tana Toraja and many other parts of the world, the dead are anything but absent.

The Bible sternly cautions against any such deliberate invoking of the departed. Yet many people have shared with me their conviction that a deceased spouse, parent, child, was present at some meaningful moment – unsought gifts of grace. These subjective experiences tell us nothing about the life of our loved ones in the world beyond, but everything about our refusal to accept death as the wiping out of personality.

Our identities survive, universal instinct assures us; human ties forged here will be resumed hereafter. It's one of the mercies of age, I find, that the afterworld fills with familiar faces. When I first tried to picture heaven, forty years ago, its golden streets were inhabited by vague, faceless beings; today they're thronged with friends and family.

Different as the contents of each hope chest are, in this one way our hope of heaven is alike. We want to be again with those we've lost! When John and I invite others to play our heaven game, everyone's 'perfect' world-to-come begins with joyous reunions.

He and I stopped for breakfast one morning in a small town in Texas where a row of pickups parked outside a cafe promised a substantial meal – grits, biscuits, scrambled eggs, patty sausage. A large table next to ours was occupied by five or six men in caps. Soon the screen door banged open to admit a newcomer.

'*Here* he is!' one of the men called out, as they scooted chairs around to make room.

There was an emphasis in the phrase that I hadn't heard before – that stress on the word 'here'. So glad, so welcoming. *He's here at last! Things are right now! The circle's complete!*

Over the next half hour, men left the table, other men arrived. And each entrance was greeted with that same triumphant cry: '*Here* he is!'

Ever since that morning, I've pictured diners at heaven's great banquet table, looking up eagerly as each new arrival approaches.

'*Here* he is! *Here* she is!' We've been waiting for you! The wedding feast is better because you're here!

Meetings

> **Eternal Form shall still divide**
> **Eternal Soul from all beside**
> **And I shall know him when we meet.**
>
> *Alfred Lord Tennyson, In Memoriam,*
> *on the death of his closest friend*

The catechism, that distillation of Christian belief, includes in the tenets of the faith this common inheritance of hope. In that passage which describes the 'new existence', heaven is where we will not only know God in his infinite fullness, but will 'fully know and love *each other*'. To know each other again, and better than before – what a promise of fulfilment to come.

Nor will the fellowship of heaven be limited to those we've known in this life. In that realm where space and time cease to matter, the catechism continues, we will be 'united *with all the people of God*'. All the people we've wished we *could* know! What a wish list each of us could draw up. On Len LeSourd's list, St Paul. On mine, Grandmother Schindler.

Who else is on my list? To start with, those I *almost* got to know here on earth. Like C. S. Lewis . . .

It was 1963 when John and I arrived for an interview with him at The Kilns, his modest brick home in Headington, just outside Oxford, England. We parked out front, reminded the children that they'd promised exemplary behaviour, and went down the front walk to the door. 'By all means bring your children,' Lewis had written. 'I have a big garden.'

The door was opened by a tall grey-haired woman – housekeeper, secretary, nurse, relative – we never knew. 'I'm so dreadfully sorry,' she said when we'd identified ourselves. 'Dr Lewis is not well. He's had no address where he could reach you.'

We left our travel schedule and wishes for his swift recovery. But, as with Henri Nouwen's illness, Lewis was dying.

And yet . . . even when the news of his death reached us three months later, I could not shake a sense of anticipation – a kind of on-tiptoe excitement about an encounter just ahead. How silly, I told myself, to keep looking forward to something that wasn't going to happen! Heaven played no part in my thinking then; I felt I was reacting like a child who won't accept 'No'.

But I've had the same sense of continuing expectation after other disappointments since then. About Nouwen. About others whose schedules never worked out with ours. *We have a date!* that inner voice persists. *We're going to have a special time together!*

I think now that it's the sort of eager anticipation we're meant to have about all those meetings an earthly lifetime can't encompass. Beloved figures like Lewis and Nouwen, of course, will have millions waiting to meet them. If heaven ran by an earthly clock, there'd be long lines stretching from their doorways. But heaven's 'time', I suspect, is very different from ours – not only endless, but simultaneous. 'Yes, I'm free to see you right now,' Lewis will say to me and to all the others – and meanwhile be able to close his door and savor his cherished solitude. I want to ask him about solitude . . .

I can hardly wait!

The Visit

**And how is it that we hear, each of us in his own native
language?**

Acts 2:8 RSV

In heaven, how many millions and millions of such meetings
are in store for us! Surely one of the graces of eternity will be the
ability to communicate across barriers of culture, language, and
millennia.

A foretaste was provided on the Day of Pentecost, when
worshippers in Jerusalem 'from every nation under heaven' were
astonished to understand the speech of men from Galilee. To
Egyptians they seemed to be speaking Egyptian, to Romans, Latin.
Medes, Libyans, Cretans, Arabs – 'we hear them declaring the
wonders of God in our own tongues!'

Whether the miracle occurred in the mouths of the speakers or in
the ears of the hearers, I believe it was a preview of the perfect
communication of heaven.

We had a fleeting glimpse of this ourselves one January day in
Czechoslovakia, when that country was still a Communist
stronghold. In a Citroën with Dutch plates, John and I had been
visiting Christians in various countries behind the Iron Curtain. In
Vienna, before we set out, we'd been given a trove of small personal
treasures – photos, letters, a few bars of chocolate – to take to an
address in Prague.

The sender was a Czech evangelist who'd had to flee his
apartment in the middle of the night, leaving behind a wife and three
daughters. Tears stood in his eyes as he explained through an
interpreter what this secondhand contact with his family would
mean to them all.

In Prague we parked the Citroën, as always, far from the Christian
household where we were headed. The car, only two years old, drew
an admiring crowd wherever in the Communist world we went, and
could draw unwelcome attention to a local family. Street directions
memorised, we set out on foot.

Alas for our effort to be inconspicuous! I was wearing a maxi-coat.
The ankle-length style had appeared years earlier in the States, but in

Prague it was apparently new, even more of a sensation than a late-model car. Pedestrians stopped and stared, drivers slowed down to look.

Nothing for it but to return to the car after a little pantomime of photographing the statue of an overweight man on an elegant horse. We drove half a mile, parked again, and set off once more, without the coat. There was no feeling at all in my legs by the time we reached the address and climbed to the apartment on the third floor. To our immense relief, the door opened to our knock. If the family had been out, we could scarcely have left a note on the door for all to read, even if we'd had a language in common.

But the wife and the youngest daughter, age nine, were home. Their excitement at receiving the few small things we'd brought was wrenching to see. As the woman served us a coffee-coloured drink, she pressed us for every detail we could remember about her husband's health and spirits. She gave us a hundred oral messages, as well as a hastily written letter, to take back to him. The girls' school reports, photos of a nephew's baby, small all-important family news.

Outside again, John insisted I wear his coat back to the car. 'What happened in there?' he asked through chattering teeth. 'What did she say? What did you say?'

I looked at him in surprise. 'But . . . you were there,' I said. 'You heard everything.'

'I heard a lot of excited conversation. It sounded like German.'

We stopped, oblivious for a moment to the cold, and stared at each other. I don't understand German, let alone speak it. Yet for almost an hour, the woman and I had somehow been conversing.

It was a little gift of God, John and I decided, to this family whose faith had cost them so much. But to us, too, it was a gift – a hint of what may be a normal encounter when spirit meets spirit, and the curse of Babel is undone.

Embarkation

My desire is to depart and be with Christ, for that is far better.
Philippians 1:23 RSV

Christians share another hope – more fundamental even than that of meeting one another, which after all is common to many religions. To us, to 'go to heaven' means above all, to be with Jesus.

In 'Crossing the Bar', that beautiful meditation on his own death written at age eighty, England's poet laureate, Alfred Lord Tennyson, likened death to setting out to sea. This poem, he stipulated, was always to be placed at the end of any collection of his works. In its last two verses – the final word, therefore, that Tennyson wished to leave with every reader – he looks forward to that most important of all reunions.

> Twilight and evening bell
> And after that the dark:
> And may there be no sadness of farewell
> When I embark;
>
> For though from out our bourne of Time and Place
> The flood may bear me far,
> I hope to see my Pilot face to face
> When I have crossed the bar.

In the 1970s I wrote a book about a young man who came to the very brink of that sea. *Return from Tomorrow* recounts the experience of George Ritchie who, in 1943, at the age of twenty, was pronounced dead of influenza in an army hospital in Texas. In the more than ten minutes before his heart started beating again – a medical 'impossibility' – he had an experience so vivid and detailed that it launched three decades of life-after-death research.

Unlike John's and my heaven game, George's vision of another world was completely unsought. Since the book appeared, other Christians have shared similar experiences with me – none of them intentional. Images of the afterlife catch these people by surprise, in fact are usually contrary to their previously held ideas.

Their reports are no more 'factual' of course than those of any subjective experience. But subjective experiences have their own truth. George Ritchie – Dr Ritchie by the time I knew him, a medical doctor and psychiatrist – has based his entire life, his choice of career, his extensive volunteer work, on those few minutes spent in a different kind of consciousness.

He was absolutely sure – 'surer than I am that I'm sitting here with you right now,' he'd say – that he'd spent those moments with Jesus. Like John's experience in the recovery room at Memorial,

Jesus came to George as light. 'Like a million welders' lamps all blazing at once,' George said. *I'm glad I don't have physical eyes,* he remembers thinking. *That light would destroy the retina in an instant.*

'The light was a Man, and this man loved me unconditionally. He knew every unlovable thing about me, every mean, selfish thought and action since the day I was born, and loved me anyway.'

Jesus' total knowledge, George went on, was simply an observable fact.

For into that room along with His radiant presence had also entered every single episode of my entire life. Everything that had ever happened to me was simply there, in full view, all seemingly taking place at that moment.

Thousands upon thousands of simultaneous happenings. How this was possible, George didn't know. He saw himself in a classroom at the University of Richmond before enlisting in the army. And at the same time – 'there was no earlier, no later' – saw his own birth and the ill and dying young mother he'd never known. He watched himself go forward at a church service at age eleven to ask Jesus to be his Lord – and watched churchgoing swiftly became a dull routine.

Illuminated by the same all-seeing Love were 'future' events, fragments of the life that follows earthly death. It was only the outskirts of heaven he was shown, George believes: a region where men and women seemed engrossed in self-forgetful tasks of many kinds.

What strikes me most about all these near-death experiences, however, is not the details, but the emotional response of the individuals to whom they occur. The 'dying' person, revived by medical intervention, is grief stricken at leaving the glorious realm he seemed to be entering. He fights his enforced return to an existence drab and dull by comparison. He pleads to stay with a presence so overwhelmingly loving that even the closest earthly relationship seems a mere shadow of the real thing.

Fond husbands, mothers with small children, young people with beckoning careers – people with literally everything on earth to live for – want only to go back to the heaven they've glimpsed however briefly. 'I cried out to Jesus not to leave me,' said George, 'not to abandon me in this dark and narrow place!'

It's so completely the opposite of the usual view – earth the sunlit realm, death the dark one – that I'm struck by the universal agreement of Christians who've stood at that threshold. Are their experiences simply the result of illness or trauma? Drug-induced delusions, perhaps, or a delirium caused by fever? They themselves, at least, say no. For the rest of their earthly lives, they continue to believe in a bright afterworld no skepticism of their hearers can tarnish.

The Saint and Brother Leo

I will forgive their iniquity, and I will remember their sin no more.

Jeremiah 31:34 KJV

And into this bright heaven, who is admitted? Everyone? An elect few? Christians only? Good people only?

After *Return from Tomorrow* was published, a number of readers wrote to challenge me with such questions. Questions far beyond my ken! Even as respected a Christian theologian as Henry Ward Beecher, that nineteenth-century champion of freedom for slaves and votes for women, would venture no opinion on who goes to heaven.

'I'll probably have three surprises there,' he said. 'To find people I never expected to see among the elect. To look in vain for some I was sure would qualify. And the biggest surprise of all – to find myself there!'

In that realm whose signature is surprise, the population will probably astonish us all. That Christianity is the Way to heaven for me, I do not doubt. That in Jesus are many ways, I suspect. Ways where in his limitless humility he works unrecognised. Such theological depths I happily leave to those qualified to plumb them; the only one whose eligibility for heaven need concern me is myself.

When I first became a Christian, 'sin' was as novel a concept to me as 'salvation'. As I slowly grasped its import, my misdeeds and failings loomed as impassable roadblocks on the journey so recently begun. I discovered the church's traditional list of 'seven deadly sins' and pasted it as a checklist to the inside cover of my brand-new Bible.

Pride

Covetousness

Lust

Anger

Gluttony

Envy

Sloth

Struggling with new self-imposed standards of behaviour, I could convict myself of several of them any day of the week.

I would repent, try harder, fail once more. The only thing that has changed through the years is my attitude toward this dismal record. What I began to notice was that those who'd walked this Way longest were also the ones most conscious of their own sinfulness.

And least troubled by it.

'No one is good but God alone,' Jesus told a young man who wanted to lead a blameless life. And for these mature souls, God's goodness was enough.

One of my favourite stories about St Francis records his response to a companion who feared he wasn't good enough to get into heaven. 'I still have not attained purity of heart,' Brother Leo lamented.

'And what is purity of heart?' asked Francis.

'It means to have no sins or faults to reproach myself for.'

'But Leo,' the saint replied, 'we will *always* have something to reproach ourselves for.'

'That's why I despair,' said Leo.

'Leo, don't be so preoccupied with yourself! Turn and look at Jesus. Rejoice that he is your Friend and Saviour.'

'Still,' Leo insisted, 'God demands our effort.'

'Certainly,' said Francis. 'But holiness is not a personal achievement. It is an emptiness you discover in yourself. Instead of resenting it, you accept it and it becomes the free space where the

Lord can create anew. To cry out, "You alone are the Holy One, you alone are the Lord," that is what it means to be pure of heart.'

The Wooden Door

> This side of eternity, we will never unravel the good from the bad, the pure from the impure. But what I have come to see is that God is big enough to receive us with all our mixture. We do not have to be bright, or pure, or filled with faith, or anything. That is what grace means, and not only are we saved by grace, we live by it as well.
>
> *Richard Foster*

To discover our emptiness . . . To discard those extravagant expectations of ourselves. To accept the Way God has provided, rather than trying to forge our own route, however virtuous-seeming.

To 'sin', said St Augustine, is to wander from this Way that leads to joy. His own early wanderings are described in his *Confessions*. This man whose writings are second only to the Bible itself in their influence on Western Christianity, started out as a Manichaean, a sect that believed that the universe was ruled by two eternally warring natures, one good, one evil. The human body belonged to the evil side and was therefore despised by 'spiritual' people.

When Augustine converted to Christianity, he rejected this dualistic picture. God is the sole creator, he declared, and everything he made is good. As for evil, it was merely a corruption of something good, like a hole in a piece of cloth, which has no existence of its own. Yes, he concluded, human nature suffers this corruption, but our own efforts at purity cannot put it right, as the Manichaeans thought. God's grace alone keeps us on the path to heaven.

The New Testament word for sin is *hamartia,* an archer's term for 'missing the mark'. Not the commission or omission of particular deeds, but being off target. Failing to do God's specific task for me alone at a given moment. Failing to be Zuysa. Failing to be Tib. No matter how praiseworthy an action, if it wasn't in his design for me, I've missed the mark.

Such sins, if I kept score, would far outnumber my bull's-eyes! I don't keep score, though. The more I know of God, the less my focus is on my own efforts, the more on the grace about which Augustine wrote so compellingly.

Near the end of that gruelling pilgrimage route from Paris to Santiago de Compostela comes the most demanding stretch of all. For John and me in 1999, crossing the Cantabrian mountains meant no more than a day in the car on a winding road. For the medieval foot pilgrim, though!

For him it had already been a trip of many months, across swollen rivers, bandit-infested forests, the snowbound Pyrenees, and an endless arid plateau. Now before the exhausted traveller loomed this second, even steeper chain of mountains.

On their eastern slope, at the start of the long ascent, is the town of Villafranca del Bierzo. And there John and I discovered a tiny pilgrimage church standing forgotten in a weed-choked field. It was raining as we picked our way around it through the wet grass. The church was locked tight, a squat grey-stone structure with mere slits for windows and what must be a very dark interior.

What we had come to see, though, was on the outside. The north wall of the little building is pierced by an arched doorway of weathered wood. To the foot-weary traveller of long ago, this was the gate of heaven.

It is the Puerta del Perdon, the Door of Pardon. Any pilgrim too old, too ill, or too lame to complete the last most strenuous seventy-five miles of the trek, could step through this door and receive all the blessings of those who made it to Compostela.

A door of pardon . . . the journey accounted complete, even for those of us who fall short. *For every imperfect traveller,* I thought, standing in the rain that afternoon, *what a symbol of hope!* I added it to Father Brinkerhoff's closet and Becky's smile in my mental picture of heaven. No pearly gates at heaven's entry! I see instead a scarred wooden door, hear a voice cry as it swings wide,

'All is forgiven! Come right in!'

Thrones

Christ Jesus came into the world to save sinners – of whom I am the worst. But for that very reason I was shown mercy so that in me, the worst of sinners, Christ Jesus might

display his unlimited patience as an example for those who would believe on him and receive eternal life.

1 Timothy 1:15–16

The door swings wide, not because we've earned entry, but because Jesus has paid the awful penalty for our sins and flung it open. Even someone living as self-forgetful a life as Catherine of Siena knew her deeds could not 'earn' heaven.

'Lord,' she cried, dying in pain at age thirty-three, 'you call me to you and I come, not in my own merits, but in your mercy, which I ask in virtue of the most precious blood of your dear Son.'

Heaven, for saints as well as sinners, God's gift of grace. Costly to him. Free to us. Unearned. Undeserved.

In 1978 John and I joined hundreds of others waiting to enter Canterbury Cathedral in England for an evening service, the culmination of a week-long conference. The crowd was so large that we were admitted by number, according to where we were housed in the nearby University of Kent. John and I were in the last group to be called. By that time, every seat in the vast nave was taken, the choir stalls were full, and even the extra chairs set up in the aisles were occupied.

Ushers led some forty of us up to the very front, where on the broad steps leading to the high altar was the only unoccupied space. We sat down on stones cold with the chill of centuries, and the service began.

Every ten years Anglican bishops from all over the world gather at Canterbury for the Lambeth Conference. This was to begin the following week, and some fifty bishops had already arrived in the city. They sat on bishops' 'thrones' in a semicircle just above us, their colourful robes a bright rainbow around the altar.

The great organ played, the hymns rang among the ancient arches. My spirit soared with the music, but as the minutes passed the ice of the stone beneath me crept into my bones. I tugged my raincoat tighter and sat on my hands.

At a tap on my shoulder I turned around. The bishop seated just above us was leaning down to me. I learned later that he was Chiu Ban It, Bishop of Singapore; what I saw was a smile and an insistent gesture at the empty throne beside him. I protested, shook my head, but Bishop Chiu took my arm and pointed firmly at the throne.

And there I sat for the next hour and a half, elevated in an instant from a shiverer on the steps to a seat among the great. I was aware of curious eyes upon me. This was before there were female priests in the English church, let alone bishops. Many must have wondered why the woman in the tan raincoat was sitting with that splendidly garbed assembly.

None wondered more than I. *Was this,* I was thinking, *how our election to heaven will be?* Suddenly raised to a seat of honour not our own? Even those late to enter, lifted high? No effort, no virtue of ours involved, simply the compassion of someone greater.

Hell

God was reconciling the world to himself in Christ, not counting men's sins against them.

2 Corinthians 5:19

Something in us rebels at this undeserved favour! If heaven's an unearned gift, where's our accountability? Do we bear no responsibility for the way we live our lives? Are there no consequences for the evil we do? What about those biblical references, so beloved of medieval painters and reforming preachers, to a hell of eternal punishment?

Long before I took either heaven or hell seriously, I'd observed that artists have a much easier time depicting torment in the fiery pit than joy among the fleecy clouds. Medieval and Renaissance paintings show every barb on Satan's instruments of torture, every clawed monster and fanged demon, in hideously believable detail.

Portrayals of heaven by these same artists are not nearly so convincing. With its leaping flames and frenzied figures, hell is at least a lively place. Depictions of heaven, on the other hand, are strangely static. There stand the saints in regimented rows, gazing motionless at a solemn Christ, rigidly seated on a throne.

Every Christmas Eve John and I tune in to the service broadcast around the world from King's College Chapel in Cambridge, England. Though the other music varies from year to year, the opening hymn is always the same: Cecil Frances Alexander's haunting 'Once in Royal David's City', sung in the angelic treble of boys' voices. The last verse looks forward to heaven:

> Not in that poor lowly stable,
> With the oxen standing round,
> We shall see Him, but in heaven,
> Set at God's right hand on high,
> When, like stars, His children crowned,
> All in white shall wait around.

Waiting around. It seems to be the only heavenly activity painters and poets can envisage.

And waiting with such sombre faces! *Why,* I wondered as I learned more about the Christian faith, *should depictions of heaven be so grimly serious? Why not merrily alive?* 'If we aren't allowed to laugh in heaven,' pronounced no less a theologian than Martin Luther, 'then I don't want to go there.'

Our sober-sides picture of heaven may be a carryover from an era of lengthy sermons and Sundays when 'frivolous amusements' were forbidden. But as anyone who's been to a Jewish wedding knows, the Bible's image of heaven as the marriage supper of the Lamb evokes a feast, a dance, a celebration, a shout of joy.

Angels can fly, someone has said, because they take themselves lightly. Everlasting bliss surely includes that absorbed contemplation of the Beloved portrayed in sacred art – but also mirth, merriment, high-spirited good humour! The Banquet of the Lamb will be fun!

A Crack in the Ground

Let no one mourn that he has fallen again and again, for forgiveness has risen from the grave.

St John Chrysostom

The lack of action in celestial imagery may also stem from thinking of heaven as the end of the story, a showcase for perfected souls, rather than a realm of ongoing growth and service. We give its citizens halos or crowns or martyrs' palms, but nothing to do, their work finished forever. It's a vision not of eternal bliss, but everlasting boredom.

'Heaven as conventionally conceived,' observed George Bernard Shaw, 'is a place so inane, so dull, so useless, so miserable, that nobody has ever ventured to describe a whole day in heaven.' A life without challenge . . . It's a state of being we can't relate to.

Hell, on the other hand, has always been sadly recognisable. We live in a world of evident evil – war, disease, cruelty. We all know pain and grief; we all know our own propensity for sin and the weakness of our best resolutions. If I hope for heaven instead of hell, it's because a power stronger and more consistent than mine is conniving at the outcome!

Sixteen hundred years ago, a man wrestled with these issues and concluded that, real though hell was, it was a pitiful and defenceless place confronted with the might of heaven.

In an age of ostentation, John Chrysostom, Patriarch of Constantinople, lived frugally. Instead of spending the church's revenues on palaces and vestments, he ministered to the poor. In AD 400, shortly before he was banished by the empress for rebuking her lavish court, he preached an Easter sermon.

'Let no one fear death,' he began, 'for the death of our Saviour has set us free.' As for hell . . .

> He destroyed Hell when He descended into it.
> He put it into an uproar even as it tasted of His flesh.
> Hell was in an uproar because it was done away with.
> It was in an uproar because it is mocked.
> It was in an uproar, for it is destroyed.
> It is in an uproar, for it is annihilated.
> It is in an uproar, for it is now made captive.
> Hell took a body, and discovered God.
> It took earth, and encountered Heaven.

It's the opposite of the aggressive hell, the sweetly passive heaven, of later art. Heaven, in John Chrysostom's view, is the formidable force!

In C. S. Lewis's novel *The Great Divorce,* hell is a grey urban wilderness of nearly empty streets, since its quarrelsome inhabitants are constantly moving farther from their neighbours. Any time they choose, these lost souls can board a bus for heaven. Ascending hour after hour through an infinite abyss, they arrive at last in a land of radiant beauty. Beside its solid residents, the busload of new arrivals are frail ghostlike creatures, too weak even to bend the grass of heaven.

'You'll firm up when you've been here awhile,' the heavenly greeters assure them, trying to persuade the newcomers to stay. Most of them, however, for the very reasons that put them in hell, insist on returning there. The book's nicest touch comes when Lewis, as narrator, returns to the brink of the chasm through which he and the other passengers on the bus have ascended. The great abyss he remembers is impossible to find. From heaven's vantage point, it's an infinitesimal crack in the soil.

'All hell,' Lewis's heavenly guide explains, 'is smaller than one pebble of your earthly world. But it is smaller than one atom of *this* world, the Real World.'

Hell a tiny, insignificant place even in comparison with earth! And earth infinitesimally small, set beside heaven . . .

'Let us not look back upon the world and fancy we have given up great things,' wrote a man who in the third century gave away an earthly fortune to live in a desert cave.

Born in AD 251 to wealthy Christian parents, Antony of Egypt was twenty years old when in church one day he heard a reading from the Gospel of Mark. 'Go,' Mark records Jesus saying to another rich young man, 'sell what you have, and give to the poor . . . and come, follow me' (Mark 10:21 RSV). Antony took the command personally. For the rest of his life – he lived to be a hundred and five! – he devoted himself to prayer, fasting, and self-denial.

And to his remote cave came everyone from peasants to Emperor Constantine himself, seeking his wisdom for their worldly problems. How did Antony understand this world we're in so well? Because he looked at it from the standpoint of an infinitely greater one.

'For the whole of earth,' he said, 'is a very little thing compared with the whole of heaven.'

The Weaver

My life is but a weaving between my God and me,
I do not choose the colors He works so steadily.
Oft' times He works in sorrow, and I in foolish pride,
Forget He sees the upper, and I the underside.

Not till the loom is silent and the shuttles cease to fly
Will God unroll the canvas and explain the reason why
The dark threads are as needful in the Weaver's skillful
    hand

As the threads of gold and silver in the pattern He has planned.

On a card distributed at the Corrie ten Boom House, Haarlem, The Netherlands

Antony looked at earth from a larger perspective.

In her suitcase, Corrie ten Boom carried a little piece of handcraft to illustrate the two different viewpoints. It was a scrap of cloth, embroidered with multicoloured threads – red, purple, black, metallic gold. Displaying it before an audience, she would explain that it represented the glorious life awaiting us in the next world. Puzzled faces would look back at her. The cloth showed only an untidy tangle of snarls and loose threads.

'Oh, I forgot!' Corrie would exclaim. 'You're seeing it from the wrong side!'

Turning the cloth around, she'd hold it up again. From 'heaven's side' it revealed a magnificent crown, the design God was weaving for eternity with the seemingly mismatched threads of an earthly lifetime.

I first saw this little visual aid as Corrie was unpacking her bags at our house. Thirteen-year-old Liz had given Corrie her bedroom, and she and I were helping Corrie put things away. The cloth, folded wrong side out, was at the bottom of the suitcase.

'What are you making, Tante Corrie?' Liz asked eagerly. Unlike her all-thumbs mother, Liz enjoys handwork.

'Oh, that's not mine,' Corrie said, picking it up. 'That's the work of the finest weaver there is.'

I probably looked as dubious as Liz did. 'I suppose it would be neater,' Corrie admitted, 'if we undid the snarls. But then . . .' with a flourish she unfolded the cloth, 'God's beautiful picture wouldn't hold together.'

Earth's side, heaven's side. Different views of the same material.

New mercies each returning day,
around us hover while we pray;
new perils past, new sins forgiven,
new thoughts of God, new hopes of heaven.

John Keble

How can we take our eyes off the snarls and see our lives from 'heaven's side'? Saints have a single answer.

Prayer.

'Prayer is the gate of heaven,' wrote Thomas Brooks, and those least upset by their trials are those who step through that gate every day.

It was David Wilkerson who introduced me to the concept of prayer not as an impulsive emotional appeal to God, but as a discipline. In 1961 John and I interviewed David for a *Guideposts* article that became two articles, then three, and eventually a book called *The Cross and the Switchblade.* David was working in the Bedford-Stuyvesant section of Brooklyn, scene of heroin addiction and gang violence that was as close to hell as anything I'd been exposed to. How did he keep going, month in, month out, we asked him, without getting discouraged?

'I couldn't,' he said, 'without prayer.'

He prayed with pimps and the pushers and the gang warlords?

Yes, if possible, he said. But what he meant, he explained, was the two hours he spent in prayer each morning before he set out.

Two hours?

We had some idea by then of the gruelling pace David maintained, following him about the city as he went from hideout to jail cell to street corner. At home were demands on a husband and father. Why would he take two hours from a schedule like his?

Because if he didn't, he said, the other hours would be wasted. 'I can only see one step ahead. God sees the end of the road.'

After the book was finished, we kept up with David, visiting Teen Challenge centres around the country and the world, as the road led places none of us could have imagined. Later we stayed with him and his wife, Gwen, at the Texas ranch where they brought inner-city kids to learn new lifestyles. And each time we got together we'd ask, 'David, are you still praying two hours a day?'

The answer was always yes.

Then in 1986, David and Gwen moved back to New York to work in Times Square, then the heart of the city's pornography and prostitution trade. As he pursued his vision of a church in that place, we asked as always, 'Still sticking to that two-hour daily prayer time?'

And for the first time, David answered, 'No.'

Uh-oh, I thought. By then John and I had watched too many ministries go wrong in just this way. An overambitious goal, a leader caught up in the pressure to achieve, neglecting his spiritual life. Temptations, greed – an all-too-human pattern.

'No,' David went on, 'here in Times Square I couldn't possibly get by on only two hours of prayer.'

Nowadays, he said, he was praying three and four hours a day.

As we watched David transform a Broadway theatre into the Times Square Church where thousands worship each week, and the entire area become the family-friendlier place it is today, we thought we caught glimpses of an embroidered crown there in the streets of New York.

Bodies

> Death is a dialogue between
> The spirit and the dust.
> 'Dissolve,' says Death; the spirit, 'Sir,
> I have another trust.'
> Death doubts it, argues from the ground.
> The spirit turns away,
> Just laying off, for evidence,
> An overcoat of clay.
>
> *Emily Dickinson*

It was the Sunday morning Bible study at St Mark's led by Rector Bill Heffner. The Scripture appointed for that day was 2 Corinthians 5:1. Our study group was using The Living Bible:

For we know that when . . . we die and leave these bodies – we will have wonderful new bodies in heaven.

'Now of course,' Bill began, 'when the Bible speaks of the "body" we will have in heaven, it doesn't mean the word literally.' The resurrected 'body', he went on, is a spiritual entity – our individual identities that live on after death.

In the sanctuary an hour later, the assistant rector, Bill Rhodes, who hadn't been present in the Bible class, mounted the pulpit to give the sermon.

'Let's not make the common mistake,' he cautioned, 'of spiritualising the concept of the resurrection.' When the Bible promises that the body will be raised, he said, it means just what it says. We will have bodies – 'transformed, glorified, made perfect' – but bodies nonetheless.

Two seminary-trained men in the same church on the same Sunday. Two views of heavenly existence. To me it said not that one was right, the other wrong, but only that the heaven they both believed in is very big. Larger, more multidimensional than we can perceive from 'the wrong side'.

What form will our heavenly bodies take? Even St Paul who was 'caught up', still living, into heaven, was not sure in what manner he'd had the experience. 'Whether it was in the body or out of the body I do not know – God knows' (2 Cor. 12:2).

Jesus' own resurrected body, during the forty days before his ascension, was apparently both solid – he walked with his grieving followers on the road to Emmaus, broke bread at supper – and immaterial – at the moment of recognition he 'vanished from their sight'. He seemed to partake during this time of two kinds of being at once: He passed through a locked door into the room where his fearful disciples were huddled, yet to satisfy literal-minded Thomas, invited him to touch the physical reality of his hands and side.

The *where* of heaven, too, which so preoccupied our ancestors, is no more answerable from our present vantage point than what our bodies will be like. In a smaller, earth-centred universe, people liked to assign heaven a location. The Egyptians placed the afterworld beyond the western horizon. The Greek 'Isles of the Blessed' were across the sea, though the poet Hesiod, writing in 700 BC, believed that heaven was in the sky, so high 'it would take a blacksmith's anvil nine days to fall to earth.' In Dante's *Paradiso,* the nine levels of heaven correspond to the spheres of the nine planets thought to orbit the earth; the better the soul, the higher the sphere.

Today, when we know ourselves to inhabit only one of billions of galaxies, in a universe where distinctions between 'up' and 'down' no longer hold, such speculations seem merely quaint. Heavenly logistics are probably nothing we can visualise. The Bible's own images of heaven are so wildly diverse as to suggest a reality we have no real parallels for. A city built of gemstones. A banquet. A sea of glass. A mustard seed.

Second Child

Metaphors like these are the best – probably the only – way to get at a truth beyond language. I remember my early quandary about numbers. How could God attend individually to billions of men and women! Then a few years ago I heard a story that gave me my own metaphor.

I can't remember where I heard it, just that it concerned a young mother so totally wrapped up with her first child that when she became pregnant again, she was afraid she could never love the new baby as much. 'There's just no room in my heart,' she worried over the phone to a friend in another town.

Some months after the second child arrived, the friend came to visit. The new child was obviously the delight of her mother. 'So you found room in your heart after all!'

'Not at all.' The young mother shook her head. 'There wasn't room, just as I knew there wouldn't be.'

The friend stared at her. 'Then how are you handling it?'

'I grew another heart.'

Yes! I thought. That's what it was like for me with our second child! The total love I felt for newborn Donn subtracted nothing from my love for three-year-old Scott. The new member of the family occupied his own inviolable space labelled *Donn's alone.* And when Liz arrived a few years later, so did a special heart filled only with love for her.

Not long after hearing this story, I stopped to look at a display of religious pictures in a window on Lexington Avenue in New York. One was the familiar image of the Sacred Heart of Jesus – the kind of too-sweet, too-literal Christian art that I've always especially disliked. Pleading eyes fixed on the viewer, Jesus points to his breast where a heart burns with flames of love.

Turned off by the style, I'd never asked myself what the image stood for. But that day I found myself remembering the young mother's answer. Perhaps, I thought, what's true of physical birth is true too of each New Birth. *This is the heart I grew for you alone,* the garish painting seemed to say. *Without you this heart would be empty.*

I went inside and bought the picture.

Metaphors. Efforts to lay hold of realities too big for definition. Our friend Bill Bair told us about taking a little boy to see the ocean for the first time. Seven-year-old Ted, Bill said, stood speechless on the New Jersey shore, staring out across that limitless, ceaselessly moving panorama, a million flashes of sunlight glinting from the surface. For perhaps five minutes the boy simply gazed without a word.

'And that,' Ted pronounced at last, 'is just on top.'

It's only the 'surface' of heaven we glimpse from earth – and even this as different from anything in our experience as the dynamic ocean from the fixed land where young Ted stood marvelling.

We're like the famous blind men arguing over an elephant. 'A spear,' said the man by the tusk. 'A snake,' insisted the one at the trunk. From a leg, 'a tree', the tail, 'a rope', the flank, 'a wall', the ear, 'a great leaf'.

And all were right.

The Cup of Coffee

Dear friends, now we are children of God, and what we will be has not yet been made known.

1 John 3:2

God can't show us heaven's side of the cloth yet, but we can seize on what he *can* tell us. With or without literal bodies, what kind of creatures does the Bible say we will be in the life to come? Not angels, certainly, that totally separate creation.

I have a shoe box where I keep cartoons about heaven, departed souls decked out with wings, white robes, and halos. Behind two of these comic conventions are good biblical concepts. Wings because in the next world we'll be free of physical limitations. White robes because in his Revelation, St John saw the redeemed clad in robes 'made white in the blood of the Lamb'.

But a halo above my head? A holiness of my own? Wholly good, pure, loving? Would this be a self I could recognise?

When John had his first cancer surgery, I stayed at a friend's apartment near the hospital. There were two other out-of-town guests there that week, young women about my age. I've long since forgotten their names, but never the impression they made.

Or . . . did not make. How can I describe two people who scarcely seemed to occupy the space through which they moved? They belonged to a movement based, they earnestly explained to me, on the 'Four Absolutes'. Absolute Honesty. Absolute Purity. Absolute Love. Absolute Trust. They had erased – at least, apparently, from their conscious minds – all negatives. No selfishness. No fear. No anger. No sorrow.

The world they described over the breakfast table was a million miles, not a few blocks, from the pain-haunted corridors of Memorial Hospital.

And far more terrifying.

There was one moment so uncanny I can feel the fright of it still. My third morning at the apartment, there was a soft knock at my bedroom door. I opened it to see one of the young women kindly holding out a cup of coffee. I could smell the brew, feel the cup's warmth as I took it from her. But though I could see her gently smiling face perfectly clearly, I was suddenly certain that she was not there.

I could walk straight forward, I thought, *and encounter only air.*

A person without personality. So yielding, so self-effacing, there was no identity to respond to. Eliminating negatives, she had eliminated some core of selfhood.

This can't be what our redeemed selves will be like! Their efforts at perfection had made them *less* than full human beings, is what I felt about my apartment mates. The modern-day saints it's been my delight to know – people like David Wilkerson, Dick Riley, Catherine Marshall, Corrie ten Boom, Molly Shelley – are complex, gutsy, many-faceted folks, full of contrasts and contradictions. They get angry, they get tired, they get discouraged and confused and out of sorts. They're not absolutely anything, except absolutely sure of God's strength and their own weakness.

Denying our humanity cannot build a life substantial enough to stand up to eternity. The larger life promised in Jesus must somehow incorporate the failures and pain of each of our stories. The dark threads of Corrie's embroidery.

When I look at Andrew Foster's portrait of St Paul in the church on Nantucket, I think back to that experience in the apartment. Not only the gold of heaven, in the painting, but the saint's black beard, his swarthy skin, his dark clothing, *all* seem to shimmer with light. And I recall what Andrew said about the way icons are painted. Western artists, he said, lay down the lighter tones first, then add dark ones for contour. With an icon, it's the reverse:

'The blacks and browns and purples go on first. Then the surface is built up, layer by layer, each succeeding colour lighter and brighter, until the whole picture seems to glow.'

The *whole* picture . . . 'Then shall I know,' wrote St Paul on one of the pages of the book that heaven has clothed in jewels, 'even as also I am known' (1 Cor. 13:12 KJV).

And what will he see as he looks at himself with that total comprehension? A flawless person? Or a person whose sombre shades too glow with the 'lighter tones' added by the brush of perfect understanding? Perhaps in heaven we will see ourselves, virtues and faults, joys and sorrows, in the radiance of the picture completed.

Finished Portrait

> **Blessed be the God and Father of our Lord Jesus Christ, who has blessed us with every spiritual blessing in the heavenly places in Christ, just as He chose us in Him before the foundation of the world, that we should be holy and blameless before Him.**

Ephesians 1:3–4 NASB

These verses describe the finished picture, the portrait of each of us that God has seen all along. Throughout our earthly lives, through our struggles and yearnings, through all our 'becoming', he sees us as we will eventually come to be in Jesus, for all eternity.

Artists, I've always thought, possess some of that divine farsightedness, that ability to see things that are 'not yet'. After Dad Sherrill's death, John's mother had stayed on at Union Seminary as Dean of Women. I was getting out of the car there one day when Mrs Van Dusen, wife of the seminary president, caught sight of two-year-old Liz.

'I'll do a pastel of her!' she announced.

This was not a lady you argued with. We set a date and Liz spent an itchy hour on the Van Dusen's sofa, sitting as still as a two-year-old can. At last Mrs Van Dusen handed me the finished product.

I tried to hide my disappointment. Mrs Van Dusen's work was highly regarded; everyone had told us how lucky we were to be getting an original by her. But . . . this wasn't Liz at all! It was a little blond child, pretty enough, but certainly not a portrait. Still, respecting the artist, I had the pastel framed and hung it in the TV room where, as with any familiar object, I soon stopped seeing it.

Four years later, rearranging pictures in that room, I stared at the drawing amazed. There was Liz! Liz to the last detail – eyes, cheeks, mouth, hair, even her customary expression! Liz at age six. Invisible to me in the two-year-old. Evident to eyes that saw more.

I like to think of God holding the completed portrait of each of us in his hand, as he's held it in his mind from the beginning. Looking at the portrait of the person he is creating, and finding it good.

Wall Hanging

For the Lord himself will descend from heaven with a cry of command, with the archangel's call, and with the sound of the trumpet of God. And the dead in Christ will rise first.

1 Thessalonians 4:16 RSV

It hangs on the wall outside my study where I pass it a dozen times a day, a five-foot panel of linen depicting in needlework the resurrection of the dead. High in the sky a trumpet summons the faithful, who leave their graves and soar upward to the outstretched arms of Jesus. At the bottom of the panel is embroidered, '*Jezus Messias Wederkomst*', Jesus the Messiah Comes Again.

The wall hanging is the work of an elderly Dutch lady who does needlework to raise money for Brother Andrew's current ministry to the Islamic world. It's her vision of the Second Coming when, the Bible tells us, Jesus will reappear on earth and the dead will rise. Our 'Easter Day', C. S. Lewis called it in the poem he composed as his wife's epitaph:

> Here the whole world (stars, water, air,
> And field and forest, as they were
> Reflected in a single mind)
> Like cast off clothes was left behind
> In ashes, yet with hope that she
> Re-born from holy poverty,
> In Lenten Lands, hereafter may
> Resume them on her Easter Day.

When will this Easter Day occur? When will Jesus come again? For two thousand years Christians have asked this question.

'Hereafter' is the most Lewis or anyone else can say. For the Bible also suggests that, for an individual, death and Easter may occur simultaneously. 'Today,' Jesus told the repentant thief who was dying with him, 'you will be with me in paradise' (Luke 23:43).

When will the dead arise? Maybe the *when* of heaven, like the *where* and the *how,* has no answer we can understand.

The Elixir

> **When we've been there ten thousand years,**
> **Bright shining as the sun,**
> **We've no less days to sing God's praise**
> **Than when we've first begun.**
>
> *John Newton*

Time in heaven . . . how different from earth's time it must be! It was another of my early difficulties in attempting to form a concept of heaven-before-us: *Forever* lasts so long! Such an endless stretch of years, centuries, millennia . . . with never any fewer eons ahead. Mightn't eternity come not as blessing, but burden?

Leos Janacek's opera, *The Makropulos Case,* is about a woman enabled as a result of a chemical elixir to live on and on. That was all I knew of the story as John and I parked the car in the Lincoln Center garage in New York on January 5, 1996, for the Metropolitan Opera's first-ever performance of it, with the great soprano Jessye Norman in the title role.

But Ms Norman never stepped onstage that night.

The house lights dimmed, the crystal chandeliers rose majestically to the ceiling of the four-thousand-seat theatre, and the curtains opened on a larger-than-life office setting. A lawyer's clerk, alone on stage, mused on the meaning of life as he climbed a ladder set against a gigantic filing cabinet. Ten feet up, he paused. The words he sang, as translated on the monitor at my seat, were:

'Too bad you can only live so long.'

As he finished the line, he released his grip on the ladder and fell backward. *What a dramatic opening scene!* I thought, probably along with the rest of the audience. *The fall so realistically done!*

Too realistic . . . falling too fast . . . landing on his back . . . In the sudden silence of the orchestra, it took a moment for the thud to reach our seats at the back of the huge house.

The curtains swiftly closed. The audience milled for a while in the aisles. When the announcement came, it was simply that Richard Versalle was being taken to a hospital. But Mr Versalle was dead, probably before he struck the floor.

The performance of course was cancelled. Back in our car, we wrestled all the way home with the extraordinary juxtaposition of stage fiction and real life we had just witnessed. A 63-year-old tenor who, my choir-trained husband says, had just hit a beautiful high B, dying as he sang that life is too short. In an opera about a woman who's discovered, according to the programme notes, that her life is too long.

A few days later I read the complete libretto. Elina Makropulos's age at the time of the story is three hundred and thirty-seven. If three hundred years has been an unendurable lifetime – as the dialogue indicates – what about a life lasting three thousand, or three million years! Elina has not grown old as long-lived people do on earth. It's not infirmity that destroys her desire to live; the elixir has bestowed perpetual youth. It's simply the ceaseless succession of days, no matter how enjoyable each one in itself, that eventually becomes intolerable.

If a never-ending life is a promise rather than a threat, time in heaven must be experienced in another way.

I got a hint of this other way when I visited a friend of my mother's in a nursing home in Sudbury, Massachusetts. Mother had warned me that Ahna wouldn't know me. A brilliant woman, a pioneer in the education of learning-disabled children, Ahna Fiske's memory, Mother said, had failed.

Sure enough, this accomplished lady had lost all recall, even of events only minutes old. Over and over, Ahna welcomed me into her room as though I'd only then arrived.

Otherwise, though, her observations were as keen as ever. She was clearly aware that her memory no longer served her, for she kept asking, 'Have I just told you that?' Nor had she lost any of her zest for life. As I stood up to leave, she apologised for not remembering the name I'd repeated a dozen times.

'I can't recall much of anything these days,' she said. 'I only have the moment I'm in, so I just enjoy that one.'

I only have the moment . . . As I went out to my car, I wondered if heaven's 'time' may be a little like that – except with our memories intact! As William Blake reminds us in his poem 'Eternity', to fail to live in the passing moment is to fail to live: He who bends to himself a Joy

> **Doth the winged life destroy;**
> **But he who kisses the Joy as it flies**
> **Lives in Eternity's sunrise.**

'Kissing the joy!' Not trying to hang onto it or waiting for a joy that's to come tomorrow. Perhaps if we could learn to do this, we'd have a hint of what heaven's time is like.

Perhaps we'll know 'forever' as *the moment I'm in.*

Photographs

> **No more will time be broken into bits,**
> **No summer now, no winter, all will be**
> **As one, time dead, and all the world transformed.**
>
> *Petrarch, 'The Triumph of Eternity'*

All experience present tense. This was only an abstract concept to me until, in 1989, our granddaughter Sarah Elizabeth was born. Sarah is the eighth in an unbroken line of Elizabeths, mother to daughter. Looking at the tiny face in the pink blanket at Brigham and Women's Hospital in Boston, I thought, *In a few years we'll have to reframe those photos!*

There are five of them now in a wooden frame in our living room, five Elizabeths photographed on our high school graduations. I'd often smiled at the fussy clothes, the beribboned hairdo, of my great-grandmother – and wished the camera had been invented when the first two Elizabeths were in school.

Back home from Boston, I picked up the frame and studied the pictures again. Liz's is the most recent: the long straight hair, the makeup-less look of the early 1970s. What will the style be, I wondered, when Sarah Elizabeth graduates in 2006?

Then I looked at my own graduation picture . . . and for the very first time saw it as Sarah Elizabeth's granddaughter will see it one day – a faded print from unimaginably long ago. The old-fashioned tailored jacket of 1945, the dark lipstick, the shoulder-length curls achieved at the cost of sleeping nightly on rollers. My time on earth as remote to her as *my* great-great-grandmother Elizabeth's is to me.

'It was real!' I wanted to tell that teenager of the 2050s. The war that ended two months after my graduation – dry statistics in her high school history books – was lived out day to day in the present.

Standing there holding that picture frame, 'past' events sprang to pulsing life for me. World War I . . . the Civil War . . . dry statistics in my own history books, and yet . . . *My mother,* I thought for the first time, *graduated as the First World War ended, my great-grandmother at the close of the Civil War.* I looked out the window and saw, not our driveway with the dustbin waiting to be brought in, but the farmer's field that was here before our suburban street was put through. The Indian trails that wound across this land before that. All in the present. *Like time in heaven,* I thought, *where all experience is embraced in an eternal Now.*

The Coin

The kingdom of heaven is like a landowner who went out early in the morning to hire men to work in his vineyard.

Matthew 20:1

For me it was the most uncomfortable of Jesus' parables, an episode so unfair by any earthly standard, that for years it said to me only that heaven played favourites. Of all my puzzlements as I tried to envisage heaven – so many of us to attend to! eternity so long! – none perplexed me more than this seeming lack of justice.

At 6:00 a.m. the landowner signs men on for a twelve-hour day, agreeing to pay each one a denarius – a small coin worth about twenty cents, the standard daily wage at the time. It's hot, backbreaking work and around 9:00 the owner recruits additional help. At noon he hires still more workers; at 3:00 he does the same. Finally at 5:00, with the weather cooling and only an hour left in the workday, he hires the bunch who've been standing around doing nothing, and sets them digging and hoeing too.

At 6:00 p.m. when they all line up to be paid, these johnny-come-latelies, whose hands are barely soiled, are each given a denarius! The weary full-day toilers are jubilant: With so generous a boss, they're sure to get a big bonus. But when their turn comes, they too each get one denarius. Not only does the landowner make no excuses for treating all alike, regardless of their contribution, he reproaches these exhausted men for supposing they deserved anything more.

For me, as I say, it was a parable that rankled. Was Jesus really saying that God, the 'landowner' of the story, will not reward lives of sacrifice in his service? I'd think of the Christians I was meeting around the world in the 1960s and seventies, people whose faith was incalculably costlier than mine. The family in Prague. Christians in Cuba who'd turned down offers of asylum in the U.S., to stay where they were needed. Members of houses churches in China, where simply to possess the Bibles John and I were carrying in was to risk arrest.

And of how I would make a few notes about their experiences . . . and walk away. Back to my comfortable church, my shelf filled with Bibles. Back where writing Christian stories took no courage.

I'd think of our friend Frank Alarcon, who gave up his job with the post office in El Paso to live across the border with the ragpickers on the Juarez dumps. Would Frank, in the next world, receive no greater compensation than someone like me?

The missionaries and martyrs down through the ages, the twelve-hour-day workers, would they really receive only a denarius like the rest of us?

I remember the morning when this seeming injustice cried out for an answer. John and I had just come back from another visit with Frank Alarcon in the floorless, windowless hovel he's pieced together from scraps of metal and wood in order to share the lives of the people he serves. Frank, it's true, in his lean-to on the dump, is one of the happiest people I know. Still, when he gets to heaven I wanted Frank to have an extra-stately mansion!

Where's your justice, God! I asked. And as I did, that morning, an answer came. I knew, all at once, what the denarius stands for.

That little coin is all there is.

Once more Jesus is trying to convey to his disciples the nature of heaven. *How* and *where* and *when,* he cannot tell them, just that they will be with him. He will give them himself – more is impossible. In him they will possess all things. They will know the Father as he does. For ever and ever they will know the perfect joy of heaven.

Though I've worked only an hour in the cool of the day, this much is offered me! The reward for those who've laboured heroically and long can be no more.

Journey's End

> Yea, through life, death, through sorrow and through
>   sinning,
> Christ shall suffice me, for he hath sufficed;
> Christ is the end, for Christ was the beginning,
> Christ the beginning, for the end is Christ.
>
> *F. W. H. Myers*

It was the eve of the crucifixion, the last night of Jesus' earthly life. As he sat at the table with his disciples, he tried to reassure them that they would be together again.

'In my Father's house are many rooms.' He was going on ahead to make ready so that one day they could inhabit this house with him. 'I will . . . take you to myself, that where I am you may be also. And you know the way where I am going' (John 14:2–4 RSV).

Thomas, a man with no patience for mysteries, objected. 'Lord, we do not know where you are going. How can we know the way?'

And Jesus answered, 'I am the way . . .'

As John and I were retracing the ancient road to Santiago de Compostela, we'd encountered what we took to be a medieval stone carver's mistake. In the Spanish city of Estella, founded in 1090 to care for footsore pilgrims passing that way, I spotted some writing over the entrance to a church. In the weathered stone I could just make out the faint raised shapes of the *Alpha*-and-*Omega,* first and last letters of the Greek alphabet, and a common symbol of Jesus. 'I am the Alpha and the Omega,' he declares in the Book of Revelation, 'the first and the last, the beginning and the end.'

'Look,' I said to John, 'they've got them in the wrong order!'

The mason had turned them around, *Omega*-and-*Alpha.*

We chuckled at the error, though it was perfectly understandable; most people back then were illiterate even in their own language, let alone Greek.

Then in Santiago de Compostela ten days later, outside the splendid cathedral that marks the end of the long pilgrimage, I stood staring up at another door. Above the cathedral's ornate south portal the oddly ordered letters were unmistakable. *Omega*-and-*Alpha.*

A mistake would never have been allowed to go uncorrected here! The reverse order must be deliberate. Why?

At Compostela, the pilgrim had not only reached the end of his journey, he'd reached the end of the then-known world. A few miles beyond the town, a rocky promontory called *Finisterre,* 'the end of the earth', juts into the grey Atlantic. John and I bought picnic makings from a stall near the cathedral and took them to some rocks overlooking the sea.

Vast, immeasurable, an ocean of unknowns. For most of human history, no one could say what, if anything, lay beyond that horizon. Was *Omega*-and-*Alpha* a message about reaching the end? The limits of our knowledge? The end of a life? Did it say that the end of one journey means the start of another?

'I say that the tomb which closes on the dead, opens to them the sky,' wrote Victor Hugo a year to the day after the drowning death of his nineteen-year-old daughter. Crushed by his loss, for twelve months he'd written nothing at all, ending his silence on that anniversary day with his triumphant statement of faith: 'What down here we take to be the end, is only the beginning.'

The German theologian and pastor Dietrich Bonhoeffer agreed. 'This is the end,' he said on April 8, 1945, the night before he was taken from his prison cell and hanged for his opposition to the Nazis. 'And for me it is the beginning.'

Omega-and-*Alpha*. Jesus not only 'the first and the last', but 'the last and the first'. Jesus the end of our earthly pilgrimage. But Jesus also the starting point of a larger journey.

Like the medieval pilgrim staring out across an uncharted sea, none of us can see beyond that horizon. But we can hear him say to us, as he said to Thomas, 'You know the way.'

The Good-bye

Remember all who have died in the peace of Christ, and those whose faith is known to you alone; bring them into the place of eternal joy and light.

Book of Common Prayer

I stood on the shore of that uncharted sea as the end neared for my earliest friend, Mea Ivimey.

By then, Mea had been in the county home for the aged more than three years, unable to speak, increasingly unresponsive. Sitting by her bed on my visits, I would wonder about her faith. What did she feel, life ending as it began, in a public institution? Did she think about the orphanage in England? Did she still dream of a *pied à terre* – even, perhaps, of heaven as the place where it had been waiting for her all along?

Mea had resisted all my attempts to talk about the Way that I had found. It seemed unfair, now when she could not protest, to force my viewpoint on her. Still, sitting at her bedside, caressing a blue-veined hand, I would struggle for a way to put the truth so she could hear it. I told her that God wanted to be the father and mother she had lost, a husband who would not desert her. Whether she understood, whether she even heard, I could never tell.

In the autumn of 1978, John and I headed overseas again. Suspecting that Mea would not be alive when we returned, John came with me two days before we left, for what did, indeed, turn out to be the last visit.

Mea was asleep, as usual, a little bit of lunch drying around her mouth. It was awhile before she opened her eyes, still longer before they focused on us. A year earlier, to prevent the spread of gangrene, her left leg had been amputated. She looked so small, lying there in the pink nightie I'd given her for her birthday, her single leg a too-narrow ridge beneath the sheet. At eighty-eight she still had that ivory-smooth complexion. One of the nurses had put a little rouge on her cheeks.

As always in the three years since she'd lost the power of speech, it was an awkward, unsatisfying time, John and I making all the conversation. We'd brought a vase of greenery from our backyard. Years earlier Mea had given me a cutting of 'proper English ivy', which I'd planted outdoors, where it had swiftly taken over the flagstones of the patio, the legs of the picnic table, and the side of the house.

I fussed with the ivy; John told her about our writing assignment in France. Finally it was time to go. 'Before we leave, Mea,' John said, 'will you let us pray with you?'

Poor lady, she couldn't say no. Standing on either side of her bed, we each took a limp unprotesting hand and reached across her to hold each other's free hand. We couldn't say what we'd really been praying since the removal of her leg – that she be allowed to die without further pain – so since John was silent, I mumbled something about Jesus being a friend who never had to say good-bye.

I finished, and still John said nothing. He told me later that when he'd opened his mouth to pray he'd started to sob deep inside himself, his throat so constricted that no sound came out.

An image formed in my mind as the three of us made our silent circle of hands. I saw Mea comforted on Jesus' lap, as she'd so often cradled lost and lonely cats.

Suddenly, breaking into this picture, came a wail from the bed. Mea was sobbing wildly, noisily, explosively, face crinkled like a child's. After the years of silence the sudden eruption of sound was stunning. On and on went the wordless cries.

Just as suddenly they stopped, and her eyes opened. And over her face, which had been so expressionless, spread a glorious smile. Then, abruptly, more frantic, heartbroken sobs. Another ecstatic smile. Three times this same sequence.

Amazingly, no hospital staff appeared during any of this, though Mea's cries must have been heard the length of the corridor. Afterward her eyes closed, and for a few minutes she seemed to be asleep. Then they opened, brilliant blue, placid, looking straight at me, but whether with recognition I couldn't tell. At last we bent down, kissed her, and said good-bye.

At the doorway we turned once more and waved. Mea's left hand stirred, and I thought it lifted a fraction of an inch. And I heard her voice, as clearly as I'd ever heard it.

'Good-bye until the morning.'

Over and over, in the more than twenty years since that moment, I've gone back in my mind to that room. What was taking place as John and I looked on uncomprehending? A heavenly dialogue we could not hear? Jesus, unseen by us, coming to claim one of his own? Certainly if John had not been with me that afternoon, I would have doubted my ears. Would have convinced myself, by now, that I hadn't heard what I did. That it was imagination, a wish.

Neither he nor I had spoken a word that day until we reached the parking lot. Then I'd turned to him. 'What did you hear?' I asked.

And he said, 'I heard, "Good-bye until the morning."'

When our reunion will be, in that morning light, in what kind of landscape, joined by what other friends and family, I can only guess.

Good-bye, God-be-with-you.

God watch over us all until that dawn!